Ivan the Terrible

KINOfiles Film Companions
General Editor: Richard Taylor

Written for cineastes and students alike, KINOfiles are readable, authoritative, illustrated companion handbooks to the most important and interesting films to emerge from Russian cinema from its beginnings to the present. Each KINOfile investigates the production, context and reception of the film and the people who made it, and analyses the film itself and its place in Russian and world cinema. KINOfiles also include films of the other countries that once formed part of the Soviet Union, as well as works by émigré filmmakers working in the Russian tradition.

KINOfiles form a part of KINO: The Russian Cinema Series.

1   *The Battleship Potemkin*
    Richard Taylor

2   *The Man with the Movie Camera*
    Graham Roberts

3   *Burnt by the Sun*
    Birgit Beumers

4   *Repentance*
    Josephine Woll and Denise J. Youngblood

5   *Bed and Sofa*
    Julian Graffy

6   *Mirror*
    Natasha Synessios

7   *The Cranes are Flying*
    Josephine Woll

8   *Little Vera*
    Frank Beardow

9   *Ivan the Terrible*
    Joan Neuberger

10 *The End of St Petersburg*
    Vance Kepley, Jr

IVAN THE TERRIBLE

JOAN NEUBERGER

KINOfiles Film Companion 9

I.B. TAURIS
LONDON · NEW YORK

Published in 2003 by I.B.Tauris & Co. Ltd
6 Salem Road, London W2 4BU
175 Fifth Avenue, New York NY 10010
www.ibtauris.com

In the United States of America and in Canada distributed by
St Martin's Press, 175 Fifth Avenue, New York NY 10010

ISBN 1 86064 560 7

A full CIP record for this book is available from the British Library
A full CIP record for this book is available from the Library of Congress

Library of Congress catalog card: available

Set in Monotype Calisto by Ewan Smith, London
Printed and bound in Great Britain by MPG Books Ltd, Bodmin

Contents

List of Illustrations   vi
Acknowledgements   vii
Note on Transliteration   viii
Production Credits   ix

Introduction   1

1   Production History   13

2   Analysis   25

3   Synopsis   136

Further Reading   144

Illustrations

1 Eisenstein with his parents.   5
2 Ivan's Coronation.   29
3 Fear and suspicion on Ivan's deathbed.   36
4 Ivan's death hood.   37
5 The 'Eye of the State'.   38
6 Alexei offers his son, Fedor, to Ivan.   42
7 Finale of Part I.   44
8 Cannoniers Foma and Erema, deleted from Kazan episode.   45
9 The Oath of the *Oprichniki*.   47
10 First blood: Ivan watchful, threatened, vengeful, doubtful.   53
11 The dance is in full swing when we enter.   59
12 'Aren't we bound by other blood, spilled blood?'   61
13 Ivan tests Staden with mockery and threats.   65
14 Ivan's repentance.   67
15 Alone? The Finale of Part III.   69
16 For the Great Russian State.   73
17 Eisenstein and his father.   82
18 Young Ivan waits in the womb-like hallway.   88
19 Fedor as 'Ersatz Anastasia'.   95
20 Ivan rises above the feast as a Superman.   96
21 Angel of the Apocalypse.   103
22 Surveillance.   107
23 Maliuta, dressed in boyar brocade.   109
24 Ivan chooses death.   113
25 Ivan paired.   118

Acknowledgements

Writing about Eisenstein would be reward enough in itself, but *Ivan the Terrible* has also brought me into the company of a group of remarkably gifted and generous scholars. Thanks first and foremost to Richard Taylor for inviting me to write this book and then waiting patiently for its completion. I am grateful to Ian Christie, Oksana Bulgakowa and Håkan Lövgren for their conversation and support early on. Yuri Tsivian, Denise J. Youngblood, Judy Coffin, Louise McReynolds, Valerie Kivelson and David Brandenberger have all read versions of this text and offered countless improvements.

Heartfelt thanks to Charters, Max and Joel Wynn for accepting Eisenstein's intrusion and my distraction in their lives; and to Max and Joel, extra credit for finding the Eisenstein moments in *Monty Python and the Holy Grail*. Rick Campa helped keep my heart and spirit intact during some hard times; I hope he will be pleased to find some of what he taught me in the pages that follow. I am grateful to the reading room staff at RGALI for their efficient help and to IREX and the University of Texas at Austin for funding my research.

Over the years Naum Kleiman has offered me his knowledge, encouragement, insight and friendship; so, for his immeasurable gift to Eisenstein scholarship and for the sheer pleasure of our conversations, I dedicate this book to him.

Note on Transliteration

The transliteration system used in this study aims for readability in the text and accuracy in the notes. I follow the Library of Congress system but in the text I have given common names in common forms, dropped hard and soft signs, and simplified endings (e.g., Meyerhold, Evstafi and Dostoevsky in the text, Meierkhol'd, Evstafii and Dostoevskii in the notes).

Production Credits

Part I
Produced by Central United Film Studios (TsOKS), Alma Ata, and
Mosfilm, Moscow
Première: Bolshoi Theater, Moscow, 30 December 1944
General release: 16 January 1945

Part II
Produced by Central United Film Studios (TsOKS), Alma Ata, and
Mosfilm, Moscow
Release prohibited by Central Committee resolution, 5 March 1946
General release: 1 September 1958

Producer and director: Sergei Eisenstein
Screenplay: Sergei Eisenstein
Editor: Sergei Eisenstein
Associate director: Boris Sveshnikov
Director of photography: Andrei Moskvin (interiors), Eduard Tisse
(exteriors)
Music: Sergei Prokofiev
Lyrics: Vladimir Lugovsky
Conductor: Abram Stasevich
Assistant directors: Lev Indenbom, Valentina Kuznetsova, I. Bir,
Boris Buneev
Cameraman: Viktor Dombrovsky
Sound: Boris Volsky, Vladimir Bogdankevich

Assistant editors: Esfir Tobak, Lev Indenbom
Sets: Iosif Shpinel (from sketches by Eisenstein)
Costume design: Lidia Naumova (from sketches by Eisenstein)
Costume assistant: Nadezhda Buzina
Wardrobe: Iakov Raizman, M. Safonova
Makeup: Vasili Goriunov
Choreographer (Part II): Rostislav Zakharov

Cast

Ivan the Terrible	Nikolai Cherkasov
Anastasia Romanova, Ivan's wife	Liudmila Tselikovskaia
Efrosinia Staritskaia, Ivan's aunt	Serafima Birman
Vladimir Staritsky, her son	Pavel Kadochnikov
Andrei Kurbsky	Mikhail Nazvanov
Fedor Kolychev, later Filipp, Metropolitan of Moscow	Andrei Abrikosov
Pimen, Metropolitan of Moscow, later, Archbishop of Novgorod	Alexander Mgrebov
Peter Volynets, his acolyte	Vladimir Balashov
Maliuta Skuratov	Mikhail Zharov
Alexei Basmanov	Amvrosi Buchma
Fedor Basmanov, his son	Mikhail Kuznetsov
Livonian Ambassador	S. Timoshenko
The Holy Fool, Nikola	Vsevolod Pudovkin
The Archdeacon	Maxim Mikhailov
Ivan as a child	Eric Pyriev
King Sigismund of Poland	Pavel Massalsky
Elena Glinskaia	Ada Voitsik
Evstafi	Pavel Kadochnikov
Heinrich Staden	Oleg Zhakov
Queen Elizabeth I	Mikhail Romm

Introduction

Ivan the Terrible is a film about dualism, so it is fitting that this book has a dual purpose. First it offers an analytical study of Eisenstein's great, last, unfinished masterpiece as a work of art. Second, it places the film in its historical and political context. *Ivan the Terrible* has almost always been viewed as a film whose politics were an unfortunate necessity, a bow to the Stalinist dictatorship and its artistic policy of Socialist Realism. This book seeks to redress that imbalance by showing the extensive political thinking Eisenstein integrated into the film and the ways in which *Ivan* was a product of the time and place in which it was made. My treatment is based on research in Eisenstein's personal archive, the archives of the film industry and government agencies responsible for film administration, and the memoirs and letters of people involved in making *Ivan the Terrible*. If the book is weighted towards the historical and political, the author can be forgiven on the grounds that this side of *Ivan the Terrible* has been largely neglected, especially in English. There already exist several excellent studies of the film as a work of art and, as I am writing this, Yuri Tsivian has just published a superb new book on *Ivan*, which approaches the film in ways that complement (and challenge) my own. But I bring to all of these a historian's questions of time, place and purpose: what sort of film did Eisenstein want us to see? How was it shaped by the world within which it was made? What does the film tell us about Eisenstein, the Soviet Union, and the practice of film-making there in the 1940s? And what does *Ivan the Terrible* still have to say to us?

Ivan the Terrible is a strange, complex and haunting film. Commissioned

personally by Stalin in 1941, the project placed Eisenstein in the paradoxical situation of having to glorify Stalinist tyranny in the image of
Ivan without sacrificing his own artistic and political integrity – or his
life. That he managed to create a film of great cinematic innovation,
intellectual depth *and* political critique is a testament to Eisenstein's
brilliance as a film-maker and his insight into the ravages of Stalinism on
his country and on himself.

In recent years *Ivan the Terrible* has received more attention from film
scholars than any of Eisenstein's earlier works and it has been screened,
often accompanied by live orchestral performances of its Prokofiev score,
more often than one might expect for a film of this complexity and
strangeness. *The Battleship Potemkin*, Eisenstein's 1926 classic,[1] will surely
remain the film we watch for early cinema experimentation, but *Ivan the
Terrible* should come to be seen not only as a great cinematic masterpiece,
but as a key event in the history of Soviet art.

Many viewers in the Soviet Union and elsewhere have believed that,
while *Ivan the Terrible* contained much of aesthetic interest, its content
was nothing more than a piece of Stalinist propaganda. But a careful
viewing of the film, supported by Eisenstein's own production notes and
the memoirs of people involved in the shoot, show that he was able to
use the political and aesthetic conventions of Stalinist Socialist Realism
to challenge the values and practices they enforced. The resulting film is
the work of a great artist navigating the treacherous waters of Stalinist
cultural politics, though with mixed success. It was Eisenstein's singular
genius to have understood that Stalin's perverted sense of 'leadership',
and his blind ambition, would be flattered by a portrait of power based
on brute force and the manipulation of his subjects, but only at first. In
the months after Part I of *Ivan the Terrible* was awarded the Stalin Prize,
Ivan the Terrible, Part II was singled out for public censure and banned,
not to be released until after both Eisenstein and Stalin were dead. We
will probably never know whether the politics of Part II were Eisenstein's
miscalculation, or a dangerous gamble, or perhaps only bad luck, but the
banning of Part II ended any possibility of completing the last part of
what was intended to be a trilogy.

Ivan the Terrible has always been a controversial film. Its subject,
treatment and its extremes and contradictions provoked heated responses
even before the film was released, and it has been the subject of contro-
versy ever since. *Ivan the Terrible* raises questions that should continue to
intrigue audiences now, more than fifty years after it was made. But if
the film is to be of genuine interest today, as something more than a
dated laboratory for outmoded experimentation, it must be understood

as a product of the historical context in which it was made. Contrary to much received opinion about *Ivan*, Eisenstein used the film to engage important political and social questions of his time rather than to evade or whitewash them.

Writing about *Ivan the Terrible* poses several difficulties. First, the film was never completed; it was butchered by censorship and self-censorship, and many scenes that were removed have been lost. There will never be a 'Director's Cut' of *Ivan the Terrible* and we will never know what film Eisenstein might have made in different circumstances. We have the complete screenplay, which he wrote in 1941 and published in the literary journal *Novyi mir* (New World) in 1943. But Parts I and II depart in significant ways from the published screenplay, so it provides only the roughest guide to the director's intent for the unfinished Part III.

Second, the film's plot is intentionally deceptive. Both to defeat censorship and to explore a variety of themes, Eisenstein depicts the events in Ivan's life in ways that simultaneously seem to praise Ivan as a visionary leader, to damn him as a brutal tyrant, and to sympathize with him as a tragic, divided and lonely man. Understanding the relationships among these thematic threads is one of the profound challenges this film poses.

Third, any attempt to understand the plot is complicated by a similar degree of ambiguity in regard to each of the film's characters. Ivan himself is difficult to pin down. At various times, Eisenstein identified Ivan with Stalin, with his own father, even with himself, and he saw all of these characters (including himself) as deeply divided figures, torn between contradictory desires. In any given scene it is difficult to determine which Ivan (or Ivans) we are meant to see.[2]

Fourth, in *Ivan the Terrible* Eisenstein experimented with much more than narrative and identity. The film contains the director's current thinking about the origins of personality and individual psychology, the process of artistic creativity and spectatorship, and the ways cinema might enable transcendence, or what he called *ekstasis* (ecstasy). Dense networks of repeated and inverted images, imitations of animation, strange and exaggerated gestures, masks and disguises, cross-dressing and character substitutions work together (or against each other) to form a shifting, layered series of episodes that comment on *all* of these subjects at the same time. Understanding this unusual structure and distinguishing the various conceptual strands it contains is another of the puzzles *Ivan the Terrible* presents.

Finally, writing about *Ivan* is complicated by the contradictory reception it received in the 1940s when it was produced and by the mistaken assumptions people routinely make about artistic production under Stalin's regime. Because Part I of *Ivan the Terrible* received the Stalin Prize (a kind of combination Academy Award and Presidential Medal of Honor), and Part II was banned only a few months later, many people have assumed that the two parts of the film differ radically in their portrait of the all-powerful leader, but this assumption is false.

These difficulties give the reader some indication of the almost infinite complexities involved in this remarkable film, but they have not been introduced here to scare you away. I offer contradiction and ambiguity as an invitation to appreciate this great director's powerful imagination and to enter the rich world of the film as he wanted us to: with more questions than answers and with unbounded curiosity about the complexities of art, power and human experience.

Eisenstein's Career before *Ivan*

In 1941, when work began on *Ivan the Terrible*, Eisenstein was the most famous film-maker in the Soviet Union, with an international reputation that circled the globe, and he was one of the country's most important cultural figures. But fame and power did not come easily, nor were they secure. Eisenstein's debut on the cultural scene was a spectacular one and it brought him enduring international renown, but he had a checkered career in the Soviet Union that included as much heartbreak and failure as success. Because so much of Eisenstein's autobiography finds its way into *Ivan the Terrible*, an introduction to his life follows.[3]

Sergei Eisenstein was born in Riga in 1898. The sheltered child of a stern, domineering father and a more flamboyant, fun-loving mother, Eisenstein's childhood was darkened by his parents' divorce and his mother's departure for St Petersburg. Many years later he would describe himself as an obedient child, following his father's wishes and demands. But his artistic talents were apparent at an early age and his obedience was matched by a rebellious spirit, which created conflicts that would shape the rest of his life.

Eisenstein was well educated and he read widely, one might say omnivorously, throughout his life. During the Revolutions of 1917 and the Civil War that followed he broke with his father, who died in exile in Germany. He had enrolled in an engineering school in St Petersburg before the turmoil began, but the Revolution allowed him to embark on a career first in the theater and later in the fledgling art of film. After demobilization, Eisenstein found a position with the experimental workers' theater Proletkult and he found a mentor (and another stern father) in the most important director of that period, Vsevolod Meyerhold.

1. Eisenstein and parents.

Eisenstein's first moving picture was *Glumov's Diary*, a short comic piece for what we might call a 'multimedia' adaptation of Alexander Ostrovky's *Enough Simplicity for Every Wise Man*. Between 1924 and 1929 he made four feature-length films on revolutionary themes and with revolutionary cinematic techniques: *The Strike* (1924), *The Battleship Potemkin* (1926), *October* (1928) and *The General Line* (also known as *The Old and the New*, 1929). *Potemkin* made Eisenstein world-famous, but, at the same time, he became embroiled in polemics – increasingly rancorous – with the rest of the Soviet film community over the *purpose* of cinema in 'the building of socialism'.

These intellectual battles would have profound political implications later on. Eisenstein was one of the leading spokesmen for those film-makers who believed that film should 'educate', rather than purely entertain, but he also believed that avant-garde methods could be educational in socialist society. He was disappointed when *Potemkin* failed to attract masses of viewers. Eisenstein's support for avant-garde experimentation would be used against him during the far more dangerous cultural politics of the 1930s. The cost of unpopular or even unpalatable opinions was much higher in the Soviet Union under conditions of encroaching dictatorship than in countries where freedom of speech is taken for granted. Eisenstein never joined the Communist Party, but he remained committed to various forms of democratic socialism throughout his life. In this early part of his career, Eisenstein believed that cinema should serve society and help build socialism. Such views would become petrified in the following decade and be used to criticize Eisenstein himself for failing to understand exactly how the Soviet state wanted to use cinema to serve society.

During the 1920s Eisenstein was one of the few practicing film directors to develop an important and influential body of theoretical writing about cinema. He developed the editing process called montage, which stressed the juxtaposition (or editing) of images in dramatic ways. Montage was intended to both startle viewers into an awareness of the constructed nature of the work and at the same time shape the ideas or conclusions they derived from viewing. Eisenstein has sometimes been criticized for emphasizing editing to the neglect of shot composition. In fact his early films introduced new techniques of camerawork, lighting and composition that intensified the dynamism to be found in film. Though his last two films of the 1920s, *The General Line* and *October*, were increasingly influenced by the specific demands of powerful political leaders, Eisenstein continued to experiment even as he began to accommodate himself to political reality.

Eisenstein missed the transition from the relative artistic freedom of the 1920s to the increasing state control of the 1930s because he was traveling abroad. In 1929 he went on an extended trip with his cameraman Eduard Tisse and his assistant director Grigori Alexandrov. The trio went to Europe and the United States in search of new sound technologies and with hopes for a lucrative Hollywood contract to bring revenue for the Soviet film industry. In Paris in spring 1930, Eisenstein signed a contract with Paramount Pictures and made his way to California with detours through London, Paris, New York and Chicago. In Hollywood, Eisenstein and his friends hobnobbed with the film world glitterati – Eisenstein developed genuine friendships with Charlie Chaplin and Walt Disney – but none of his three film projects was put into production. Rescue seemed to be forthcoming in an offer from wealthy socialist writer Upton Sinclair to fund a film about Mexico, *Que Viva Mexico!*.

Eisenstein's year in Mexico was one of utter delight both personally and artistically. Mexico City in the 1930s was an international cultural center, less well known, but as important and exciting as Paris, with expatriate artists drawn from around the globe. Eisenstein found the environment extremely congenial and stimulating. His old interest in anthropology was revived by his fascination with Mexican culture. He began to draw again, a practice that he would continue almost obsessively for the rest of his life. Eisenstein's drawings for *Ivan the Terrible* became the basis for the sets, costumes and characterizations as well as movements through space.

But Mexico was too much fun. Sinclair became disgruntled with filming that ran months over schedule and he was disturbed by rumors of sexual escapades. When Stalin threatened to banish Eisenstein permanently if he did not return to the Soviet Union, Sinclair seized the opportunity to pull the plug on *Que Viva Mexico!*. Eisenstein never recovered the year's worth of footage and for the rest of his life he was haunted by the loss.

The Moscow Eisenstein found on his return in May 1932 was more constricted and impoverished than the city he had left. Exhilarating ideas about art serving society had become the rigid guidelines of artistic institutions that were controlled by Communist Party bureaucrats. A paradoxical situation emerged. Eisenstein's numerous projects and proposals were turned down but he remained the face of Soviet cinema for the international film community. His unfettered polemics of the 1920s were not forgotten and he was unable to make new films to reestablish a new reputation at home. The Stalinist political culture, which encouraged public criticism and denunciation, inflamed old injuries and cultivated jealousies. At conferences and public meetings, Eisenstein was attacked not only by Party hacks, but by old friends and associates. He was criticized for being out of step, old fashioned and 'formalist', which is to say he cared more about experiments with cinematic form than with making films 'accessible to the masses'. The 1930s were a period of repeated frustration and humiliation at the hands of the film industry, in particular its chief, Boris Shumiatsky, who loathed Eisenstein. During the 1930s Shumiatsky decided which kinds of films best served Soviet society and he saw to it that few of Eisenstein's proposals would go into production.

In the meantime, Eisenstein read everything, wrote a great deal of film theory and taught. The teaching took up valuable time, but he found it enormously satisfying and ultimately useful when he got back to filming again. He was a gifted and inspiring teacher, drawing on his wide reading and famous sense of humor to draw students into the creative process.

By nature, Eisenstein was a deeply private and cautious man. He could be charming and charismatic in social situations as well as serious and demanding while working, but these were public masks; he guarded his private life. People familiar with Eisenstein through his published works and revolutionary silent films are always surprised to learn that he was famous among friends for his pranks and dirty jokes. His small circle of close friends protected his privacy and even his diaries are rarely revealing. As a result, his friendships and intimate relationships with men and women have been the subject of speculation, gossip and wishful thinking. It seems clear that he had sexual relationships with both men and women but also that these were rare and short-lived. In 1934, just after a law was passed making male homosexuality illegal in the Soviet Union, Eisenstein married his good friend and assistant, Pera Atasheva. He had at least two serious relationships with women, but broke them off when they threatened to become too intimate. About men, Eisenstein wrote only in the most diversionary manner. Records of his relationships with men are scarce and no one who knows more is talking. He had one known sexual relationship with a man in Mexico and he consulted with psychoanalysts on several occasions about his bisexuality in the 1920s and 1930s; and *Ivan the Terrible* is so suffused with homoeroticism as to indicate more than a passing interest in the subject. It is fair to say that Eisenstein's sexuality was a source of some dissatisfaction for him and that his private life in general brought him considerable pain. He suffered from periodic bouts of serious depression from the 1930s on and his health was regularly threatened by heart disease as well as influenza and chicken pox.

The political attacks on the director culminated in 1937, the height of the Great Terror, which saw the mass arrest, imprisonment and execution of prominent intellectuals, political leaders and other citizens, men, women and children. In that year, after many delays, Eisenstein was finally nearing completion of *Bezhin Meadow*, his first film since returning from abroad. Shumiatsky had the production halted, but he did not stop there. He denounced Eisenstein to the Central Committee (the highest Party institution in the Soviet Union), and then directly to Stalin, which can only be interpreted as inviting a death sentence for the director. Eisenstein left Moscow for Kislovodsk (a resort in the Caucasus) in hopes of distancing himself from the firestorm. The highest authorities decided that Eisenstein was reliable enough to allow him to continue trying to make films, and that Shumiatsky had overstepped his own authority, having published an article attacking Eisenstein that he had been explicitly discouraged from publishing. This was no petty squabble among artists and bureaucrats over the interpretation of a film. Everyone involved knew that they were playing a game of life and death. It turned out that Eisenstein had just enough support among Party members in the film industry and, more critically, on the Central Committee (whose decisions could be capricious in the extreme). Shumiatsky, on the other hand, did not accept defeat gracefully and refused to back down. In a horrifying, but typical, Stalinist reversal, *Shumiatsky* was arrested in the following year, and subsequently shot.[4]

After writing the required self-criticism, Eisenstein was given the opportunity to make a historical film. He chose Alexander Nevsky as his subject, and the eponymous result was his most popular film, with its heroic battle against German invaders. Eisenstein, however, was ashamed of it and it is generally considered to be his least interesting in technical and intellectual terms. For Eisenstein personally *Nevsky* provided a number of important political lessons, which would come in handy in making *Ivan the Terrible*. In 1937, Shumiatsky's attack on *Bezhin Meadow* had plunged Eisenstein's reputation to its lowest point and put his career as a film-maker in mortal danger. Then, suddenly, the success of *Alexander Nevsky* catapulted him to the highest of inner circles. He had finished *Nevsky* in record time, he had made a film that was patriotic, and he wrote appallingly obsequious, bombastic articles for major newspapers about it. In 1939 he won the Order of Lenin and in 1941 *Alexander Nevsky* won the newly created Stalin Prize. In a restructuring of the film industry that brought more artists to positions of authority, Eisenstein was made Artistic Director of Mosfilm, a prestigious and powerful job. But, as if to underline the capriciousness of these decisions and the fragility of his own position, *Alexander Nevsky* was withdrawn from circulation after Stalin signed a non-aggression pact with Nazi Germany and then returned to circulation when the Nazis broke the pact and invaded the Soviet Union in June 1941.

Eisenstein's life is a difficult one to categorize. He participated in the birth and coming-of-age of Soviet cinema, during the birth and coming-of-age of the Soviet Union. He adhered enthusiastically to the revolutionary utopianism of the early Soviet experiment and witnessed its liquidation by encroaching bureaucratism and authoritarianism. As an ambitious and polemical creature, Eisenstein maneuvered skillfully in the world of Russian avant-garde politics, reaching the pinnacle of that world in the late 1920s. But, as a cosmopolitan and culturally omnivorous intellectual, Eisenstein was often a victim of politically motivated or culturally narrow policies. His successes often came in spite of differences with Party and official cultural policies. He played a major role in every debate over the future of Soviet cinema in the 1920s, but as a 'formalist', Eisenstein was often entirely out of step with official policy, for which he paid dearly in the intolerant 1930s and 1940s. Though he was prodigiously well-read, his knowledge of Marxist theory was not extensive and his uses of it idiosyncratic, even at the height of his 'revolutionary period'.

As a result, Eisenstein never occupied an unambiguous political position. A highly sociable but intensely private man, Eisenstein mastered the ability to wear a variety of masks and to speak in a variety of codes in the volatile historical, cultural and personal contexts within which he operated. His films are complex and multi-layered, with deceptive narrative and visual structures. His writings are informed by Marxism but not exclusively or uniformly. His public activities are marked by cryptic utterances, command performances and an ironic use of the high-blown official rhetoric that contrasts sharply with the supple, spontaneous and passionate language of his notebooks and letters. His lifelong use of diverse and often contradictory forms of self-presentation eludes clear political identification. Neither Bolshevik nor dissident, neither Stalinist nor anti-Stalinist, neither martyr nor villain, historians and observers on the left and the right have both found reason to avoid his politics or to oversimplify them.

To further complicate matters, Eisenstein's politics changed over time. With growing knowledge and experience, Eisenstein witnessed the changing political context in sickening close-up: the end of the utopian possibilities of his youth, the closing of Soviet cultural life to the outside world, the rise of bureaucratic hacks in arts administration, the Soviet

Union's descent into authoritarianism and terror. Eisenstein's travels gave him opportunities for comparison that few members of his generation possessed. He came to see that life as a socialist artist in Moscow in 1929 differed dramatically from life as a Russian socialist in red-baiting Hollywood in 1930 and that neither could match the sympathetic community he found in the left intellectual circles of cosmopolitan Mexico City in 1931. Eisenstein was as much out of his element in Moscow in 1932 and for the rest of his life as he had been in Hollywood, but what exactly socialism meant to him and how socialist ideology was represented in his films are questions more difficult to answer than they may seem. It is especially important to remember that to have invented socialist foundation myths in Russia in the 1920s was an entirely different project than producing Stalinist propaganda in the 1930s and 1940s. Eisenstein's career cannot be measured against yardsticks that cover the whole period, the whole world, or any single ideology. As he changed, the meaning of his works changed accordingly, in and out of step with the society around him.

Ivan the Terrible would be produced in the same atmosphere of uncertainty and political reversals that he had experienced throughout his career. It proceeded in fits and starts, repeatedly in danger of being halted. But in Alma Ata, far from the center of power and under the cover of wartime conditions, Eisenstein risked making the film he wanted to make.

Notes

English translations have been cited when possible. All archival sources are located at the Russian State Archive of Literature and Art, RGALI, unless otherwise noted. The following abbreviations have been used for frequently cited works:

ER The Eisenstein Reader, R. Taylor (ed.), W. Powell (trans.), London, 1998
ESW 3 S. M. Eisenstein, *Selected Works: Vol. 3. Writings, 1934–47*, R. Taylor (ed.), W. Powell (trans.), London, 1996
ESW 4 S. M. Eisenstein, *Selected Works: Vol. 4. Beyond the Stars. The Memoirs of Sergei Eisenstein*, R. Taylor (ed.), W. Powell (trans.), London and Calcutta, 1996
KZ Kinovedcheskie zapiski
NN S. M. Eisenstein, *Nonindifferent Nature*, H. Marshall (trans.), Cambridge, 1987
NFD S. M. Eisenstein, *Notes of a Film Director*, New York, 1970

1. See Richard Taylor, *The Battleship Potemkin*, London, 2000, in this KINOfiles series.
2. Recent orchestrated screenings of *Ivan the Terrible* in the USA show a trun-

cated version of the film, which foregrounds the bizarre and tragic images of Ivan.

3. The following sketch is based on Eisenstein's writings, letters, journals; his autobiography, *Beyond the Stars*, and other sources including Y. Barna, *Eisenstein*, London, 1973; David Bordwell, *The Cinema of Eisenstein*, Cambridge, MA, 1993; Ivor Montagu, *With Eisenstein in Hollywood*, New York, 1967; Vladimir Nizhny, *Lessons with Eisenstein*, London and New York, 1962; Marie Seton, *Sergei M. Eisenstein: A Biography*, London, 1952; Oksana Bulgakowa, *Sergei Eisenstein: A Biography*, Berlin and San Francisco, 2002.

4. Leonid Maksimenkov, *Sumbur vmesto muzyki: Stalinskaia kul'turnaia revoliutsiia, 1936–1938*, Moscow, 1997, pp. 241–53.

1. Production History

In early January 1941 Eisenstein received a visit from Andrei Zhdanov, a Politburo member and Stalin's aide in charge of propaganda, the media and the arts. Nothing is known about the meeting itself, except that Zhdanov came armed with a proposal that Eisenstein make a film about Ivan the Terrible and that Eisenstein set to work on the project immediately. His early notes for the film show that he was thinking about both form and content, character and history from the very start. These first notes mention the idea of beginning shots with an uneven editing rhythm and creating discontinuities between episodes, to represent an adult's unsystematic memories of childhood. He jotted down something he read about the secrets and lies in Ivan's earliest experiences, specifically noting that Andrei Shuisky, one of the boyars whose power rested on the young age at which Ivan ascended the throne, punished an old boyar for telling Ivan about his grandfather's great power and thereby suggesting that Ivan think about his own right to rule.[1]

Throughout the spring of 1941 Eisenstein read voraciously in the available primary sources on Ivan's reign, including Ivan's correspondence with Andrei Kurbsky, the boyar whose betrayal became central to Eisenstein's plot, and the German Heinrich Staden's account of his service to Ivan as a member of the *oprichniki*. He read the nineteenth-century classic histories by Vasili Kliuchevsky, Sergei Soloviev, Nikolai Karamzin and others, and the more recent popular biography of Ivan by Robert Vipper. His reading also included Machiavelli, Shakespeare (especially *Henry IV Part I*), Dumas ('though Dumas was not what was needed'),[2] Galsworthy ('bad, very bad')[3] Goethe, Flaubert, Averchenko, Thornton Wilder, J. B. Priestley, Maeterlinck *and* Metternich. He consulted Havelock Ellis on sexuality, Rank and Freud on the psyche, J. W. Beach on modernist narrative theory, Frazer and Malinowski on ethnography, Igor Grabar on medieval art. He read works on folklore, biblical psalms, and he brushed up on his Nietzsche, Marx, Engels, Belinsky and much more. Eisenstein was permitted to write his own screenplay for the film and working with great speed he completed a first draft in April 1941. He read it to friends, including the documentary film-maker Esfir Shub, and he submitted it for official approval. The approval process dragged on for many months, during which time Eisenstein continued to revise and rewrite. It was not until 5 September 1942 that the screenplay was finally approved.[4] Official approval had to come from the Committee on Cinema Affairs of the Council of People's Commissars. The Committee offered approval only on the provision that Eisenstein cut or revise several scenes with questionable political overtones. He was instructed to omit references to Queen Elizabeth I and Ivan's efforts at diplomacy with England, to make his representatives of the Russian people more dignified, to limit attention to religious issues, to revise a scene in which one of Ivan's servitors spoke openly to the tsar and seemed 'on an equal footing' with him, to stress the positive sides of Ivan's reign, and finally to minimize the theme of Ivan's loneliness on the one hand and his manipulation of the people on the other.[5] Eisenstein agreed to all these deletions and then proceeded to ignore most of his agreement. He wrote to Pera Attasheva that only the English diplomatic theme had to go, but he still shot screen tests for that scene when production began.[6]

The negotiations over the screenplay are important because they show the extent to which the Committee on Cinema Affairs tried to interfere in the content of the film and the extent to which Eisenstein felt he could ignore their instructions. They also show the presence of dangerous political themes in Eisenstein's conception of *Ivan* from the very beginning of the project. These early readers found in the screenplay an Ivan who was demagogic and tragic, unheroic, unconstructive, brutal towards his enemies but conscience-stricken at the same time, and they found a portrait of the Russian people as easily manipulated fools. Party watchdogs expected Eisenstein to tone down the shooting script in order to make a film that could be released, but he did not oblige.

Instead, Eisenstein took care to protect himself and his film from the kinds of criticism with which he had become familiar during his roller-coaster career. He did this primarily by keeping the project in the public eye as much as possible, or at least the elements of the project that would be acceptable to Party censors. Eisenstein wrote articles for prominent newspapers about his approach to Ivan the Terrible, he had the screenplay published in Russia's premier literary journal, *Novyi mir*, and he tried to make careful choices about which state pressures to give in to. So, for example, in March 1941 Eisenstein received the Stalin Prize for *Alexander Nevsky* and was asked to write an article for *Pravda*, the Communist Party's main newspaper. The resulting article, 'The Heirs and Builders of Culture', celebrated Soviet artists for continuing 'to advance the cause of world culture' in their unique position outside the turmoil engulfing the rest of Europe. It also credits 'the wisdom and foresight of the Soviet government and Comrade Stalin', for making the Soviet Union the only country in the world where artists could still work in peace – an obvious but unstated reference to the Nazi–Soviet non-aggression pact of 1939.[7] Many Soviet artists during this period categorically refused to offer Stalin their public support and many more were appalled by the non-aggression pact Stalin signed with Hitler, but Eisenstein knew what it would take to retain the support he needed, and he chose compliance. The cost to his conscience and reputation was high, but *Ivan the Terrible* went forward. Sometime later, in September 1943, Stalin himself signed a memo stating that the way Eisenstein had represented 'Ivan the Terrible as a progressive force for his time and the *oprichnina* as his effective instrument turned out not badly'.[8]

In working on the screenplay, he reversed the strategy that had worked well for *Alexander Nevsky*: in 1937 Eisenstein had reputedly chosen to make a film about Nevsky because the lack of historical documentation about Nevsky's life would allow the film-maker to create a central character useful for his own purposes. For *Ivan*, Eisenstein employed an assistant, Lev Indenbom, to collect as much historical source material as he could find. Together they documented hundreds of historical details that would appear in the film. He hoped to publish these historical reference notes together with the screenplay, but the journal refused.[9]

In the meantime, war was coming. Eisenstein spent late spring 1941 preparing for production in the expectation that shooting would begin soon on what had become a prestige project. He was at his dacha outside Moscow on 22 June 1941 when news of the German invasion reached him. All the major film studios held emergency meetings on that first day of the invasion to decide how best to support the war effort. The Soviet government had always considered film an important means of political persuasion and during the war film-making was considered essential for maintaining morale. Eisenstein led the discussion at Mosfilm, where it was decided to make a series of short films with clear anti-fascist messages as quickly as possible. Older writers and directors threw themselves into this work, while younger crew members and actors gave up their jobs to join the army, often opening up positions for women.[10] But some young actors and technicians were commanded to stay behind to make movies. Young men like Pavel Kadochnikov, who would play Vladimir Staritsky in *Ivan the Terrible*, found it humiliating to be acting in films far to the rear while other men and women of his generation were facing live ammunition, but film was war work and the studios were given quite remarkable resources during a time of great deprivation to continue production.

In October, as the Nazis approached Moscow, Eisenstein recorded in his diary the cities as they fell and the nightly bombings of Moscow. Then on 14 October 1941, the entire Moscow film industry was evacuated to Alma Ata (now Almaty) in Kazakhstan. The evacuation was an enormous undertaking. Train journeys were slow as they passed through stations filled with mobilized soldiers and hungry refugees of all ages. In Alma Ata thousands of actors, crew and staff had to be housed in dormitories or barracks. Eisenstein complained in private about his small apartment, but he was lucky to have it. Food and fuel were scarce even before the city was deluged with thousands of artists, intellectuals and workers for the factories that turned out war materiel. The weather was balmy in October but soon would turn cold and dreary and then un-bearably hot. Eisenstein's film was put on hold, while more immediate tasks were given priority. In Alma Ata, he was involved in constructing new studio space, transferring and reopening the Central Film School (VGIK) and producing war films.

Many of the Soviet intellectuals who were dispersed to various cities in Central Asia during the war would remember those years with deeply paradoxical feelings. Despite terrible deprivations, losses, an unimaginable death toll, many people remembered the Second World War as a time of relative freedom of expression and a genuine, uncoerced, collective effort in the fight against fascism. As Dmitri Shostakovich put it, 'the war brought great sorrow and made life very hard. Much sorrow and many tears. But it had been even harder before the war, because then everyone was alone in his sorrow.'[11]

Eisenstein shared the populist patriotism, but his memories of the period are almost exclusively bitter. He hated Alma Ata. He was tor-mented by the climate, frustrated by the primitive conditions, and suffered especially from a sense of isolation. To friends who stayed behind in Moscow or who returned sooner than he, he complained in frequent letters, begging them to visit or send books. His diaries are marked with sad entries about the people he knew who were killed at the front and with the trickle of news from the terrible siege of Leningrad. He endured serious illness, exhaustion and bouts of the depression that had often plagued him in the past. Yet few who encountered Eisenstein in Alma Ata knew of his private troubles. Most people there found him congenial, hospitable and supportive. Once filming began, he could be demanding, even insensitive, but most of his cast and crew ultimately believed his demands were motivated by the deepest artistic commitment.[12] Rostislav Zakharov, the choreographer who created the 'Dance of the *Oprichniki*', saw Eisenstein as a man 'blessed with the gift of charming everyone who worked with him ... He was always cheerful and smiling, tossing out witty comments, generating an exceptionally creative atmosphere. But when necessary, he could be strict and demanding, insisting on adding necessary nuances to the execution of his vision, forcing repetitions in search of the best version.'[13] Even Serafima Birman, who played Efrosinia Staritskaia and was the most difficult member of the cast, was impressed by the loyalty and commitment Eisenstein inspired in his crew, though she frequently found him cold and unsympathetic.[14]

Despite, or perhaps because of, wartime conditions in Alma Ata, Eisenstein remained remarkably busy even before *Ivan* went into production. During the day he saw to his studio responsibilities and, in his spare time, at night, sometimes *all* night, he continued thinking about and developing ideas for *Ivan the Terrible*. An extraordinarily fertile period began in early 1942, when he began working intensively on character, plot development and shot composition. During this period he had some of his most important insights and he began making the series of remarkable drawings that he used to work out the visual style of the film. Throughout his life, Eisenstein continued to mine his previous films for ideas, long after they were finished. In the case of *Ivan the Terrible*, the production delays caused by war, evacuation, politics and other disagreements allowed Eisenstein to perform this sort of ruminative analysis while waiting for production to begin. Between 1942 and 1944 he filled literally scores of notebooks with thoughts and drawings, pushing himself to extend and clarify his conceptualization of *Ivan the Terrible*. However frustrating the delays were for him – and even more so for his cast and crew – the postponements undoubtedly deepened the film's narrative elements and enriched its formal structure.

Once the screenplay was approved in the fall of 1942, casting *Ivan the Terrible* could begin. Nikolai Cherkasov, who had played Alexander Nevsky, left his wife and baby son in evacuation in Novosibirsk to come to Alma Ata to play Ivan. Ivan's adoring servitor and last loyal friend, Maliuta Skuratov, was offered to Mikhail Zharov, a beloved comic actor (though Zharov wanted to play Andrei Kurbsky). Kurbsky, the traitor, was played by the tall, stately, sensitive actor Mikhail Nazvanov, whose first film role had been the romantic lead in one of the most well-known Russian war films, Alexander Stolper's *Wait for Me* [Zhdi menia, 1943]. Nazvanov's career had not always been so successful. In 1935, he had been a twenty-year-old novice actor at the celebrated Moscow Art Theater when he was denounced to the police for telling a political joke. He was arrested and served five years of hard labor in exile, before being released at the beginning of the war.

The young Ivan was played by Eric Pyriev, the son of another well-known Soviet director, Ivan Pyriev. Eisenstein wanted his rival film-maker, Vsevolod Pudovkin, for the Metropolitan Pimen, but Pudovkin was busy with his own film at the time. Later Pudovkin was cast as the snarling 'Holy Fool', Nikola, and Eisenstein invited Alexander Mgrebov, a stage actor in evacuation in Novosibirsk, to come to Alma Ata to play Pimen, not knowing that Mgrebov was deathly ill at that time with tuberculosis. Mgrebov later claimed that the invitation saved his life, because when Eisenstein saw the condition he was in by the time his train arrived in Alma Ata, the director used all his influence to provide Mgrebov with the best possible medical care.

The young men in the film, Fedor Basmanov and Vladimir Staritsky, were played by actors of diametrically opposed temperaments. The devilish, dark-haired Mikhail Kuznetsov who played Fedor clashed repeatedly with Eisenstein over acting method. Pavel Kadochnikov, blond and delicate-looking, became a favorite of Eisenstein from the start.

It proved much more difficult to cast the female parts, Ivan's wife Anastasia, and Ivan's major rival, Efrosinia Staritskaia. Neither role was filled until more than six months of filming had already gone by. When Eisenstein's first choice for Anastasia could not get permission to travel to Alma Ata, he tried to persuade the talented ballerina, Galina Ulanova, to take the role. She was intrigued and surprised, never having acting in a film, and agreed to pose for a series of screen tests. To Eisenstein's great chagrin, she declined the role, unwilling to sacrifice her dancing career for the amount of time the filming would take. This occurred at the end of 1943, when shooting Anastasia's scenes could be delayed no longer. The role was finally offered, on the very eve of filming, to Liudmila Tselikovskaia, who happened to be Mikhail Zharov's wife.

Efrosinia proved even more problematic. Eisenstein wanted Faina Ranevskaia and got as far as shooting screen tests, the photographs of which show a face of great power and expressiveness. But when Ivan Bolshakov, Chair of the Committee on Cinema Affairs (who had final

approval of casting choices) saw those same photographs, he saw only
Ranevskaia's 'Jewish' features and, responding to a renewed atmosphere
of official anti-Semitism, decided that she was ineligible to play a 'Russian'
boyarina.[15] Infuriated, Eisenstein gave in only after months of arguing
and stalling failed to change Bolshakov's mind. The stage actress Serafima
Birman was finally offered the role. She was not a popular choice and
when she arrived on the set she immediately provoked hostility from the
makeup and costume crews, several of the actors and the cinematographer, who took one look at her and turned away.

Eisenstein had already asked Prokofiev to write the score in 1942. After
their successful collaboration on *Alexander Nevsky*, Prokofiev was eager to
work with Eisenstein again. As soon as he finished his opera of *War and
Peace*, he put himself at Eisenstein's disposal. They would work together
sporadically, in Alma Ata and in Moscow, depending on Prokofiev's
schedule, over the next three years.

Filming finally began, after many more delays, in April 1943. Within
a few weeks a new problem arose. Since his very first feature in 1924,
Eisenstein had worked with the same cameraman, one of the best in the
business, Eduard Tisse. Tisse had accompanied Eisenstein to Hollywood
and Mexico, and his own career had been tied to Eisenstein's for twenty
years. But apparently even before shooting began, Eisenstein began to
think that he needed a new look for *Ivan*. His earlier films had celebrated
externals, dynamic movement and masses of people, but *Ivan* would be
different. Though Eisenstein never abandoned his interest in the look and
composition of the shot, *Ivan the Terrible* required dynamism that would
also be internal, psychological and individual. At least a year before
shooting began, in mid-1942, with the production stalled and Eisenstein
stuck in Alma Ata, he was seen taking long walks with Andrei Moskvin,
Russia's other 'greatest' cinematographer. They immediately found a
common language, both intellectually and temperamentally, but the situation was delicate and needed to be handled with care. Eisenstein was
especially concerned because during the war anyone with a Germanic-
sounding surname was vulnerable to arrest, and Tisse, though not German, had already been threatened by the police. Keeping him on the
production was essential. Two months after shooting began, Moskvin
was officially brought in as cinematographer for all interior scenes, and
effectively became what we call today the Director of Photography; Tisse
was retained for outdoor filming. 'With Tisse, everything was and is still
very painful,' Eisenstein would write to Pera back in Moscow.[16] Whatever
bitterness Tisse felt, he kept to himself.

Originally Eisenstein planned to shoot all of *Ivan the Terrible* in Alma

Ata, the entire screenplay from start to finish. But it quickly became apparent that *Ivan*'s complexity required more time than expected. Between April 1943 and July 1944, when the production moved back to Moscow, scenes were shot from both Parts I and II at the same time and several key scenes from Part III were completed.

By all accounts, *Ivan the Terrible* was shot under conditions that would have seemed catastrophic had the rest of the country not been at war or under siege and occupation. A shortage of electricity in Alma Ata meant that indoor filming could take place only at night, when the available fuel was not being used for industrial production. From six in the evening until eight in the morning, sometimes for weeks at a time without a day off, actors and crew were forced to stay on the set in full medieval costume and makeup. The studio was blisteringly hot in the summer and freezing in the winter (the vapor from Filipp's breath is visible in some shots). The less prestigious actors were often hungry as food supplies were scarce. And Eisenstein was an exacting director, requiring the actors to hold physically torturous poses for long periods of time, while he shot and reshot each scene. There were times when the actors had had enough. After a year of shooting, even the jovial Cherkasov could become hysterical after a long night on the set and Mgrebov was near death. Nazvanov began to feel like nothing more than a 'wooden marionette'.[17] But despite these hardships, with very few exceptions, no one complained. Eisenstein inspired his cast and crew to believe that they were engaged in a project of great significance. The director himself set an example, working harder than anyone else, with a hand in every detail, always accessible, and with a kind word or a funny joke at just the right moment, visibly placing the value of the work above his own individual comfort.

Eisenstein has a poor reputation as a director of actors and Nikolai Cherkasov is famous for complaining about the physical contortions Eisenstein forced him to perform as Tsar Ivan. But Cherkasov well understood that Ivan was the role of his life and most of the other actors describe working with Eisenstein on *Ivan the Terrible* as the chance of a lifetime. Those actors who understood what Eisenstein was trying to accomplish were in awe of the director's abilities, often felt that they were the 'co-authors' of their roles, and categorically denied the view that Eisenstein was not an 'actor's' director. Others, like Mikhail Kuznetsov (Fedor Basmanov) who had been trained by Stanislavsky or were adherents of the Stanislavsky method, found working with Eisenstein more frustrating. Kuznetsov and Birman were offended by Eisenstein's indifference to their efforts to explore the psychological essence of their characters. To have been disliked by Eisenstein cannot have been very comfortable, but his admirers seem to outnumber the discontented. Even the skeptical Nazvanov was won over when he saw the footage of his scenes and realized that, somehow, Eisenstein's peculiar style of direction had enabled him to capture the role of Kurbsky. Eisenstein's fans came from the ranks of his crew as well. According to *Ivan*'s Prop Master, Gleb Shandybin, Eisenstein 'not only knew everyone well, he treated everyone [on the set] with respect; for him there were no unimportant professions, no "table of ranks". He was attentive to the workers on the staff and the technical personnel, he valued their work and inspired them by showing that he understood the significance of their contribution to the picture.'[18]

Throughout the production process, Eisenstein had to fight with Moscow for funding, equipment and permission to keep his crew paid, fed and on the set. The studio was frustrated with the slow pace of production. Eisenstein carried on as if he knew he had enough clout to make the film he wanted to make, regardless of pressures emanating from Moscow and from actors eager to return to Moscow. By the end of 1943, after nine months of production, the film remained unfinished. When Bolshakov demanded that he speed up the production, Eisenstein threatened to write directly to Stalin to get Bolshakov off his back.[19] It was a dangerous (and audacious) step, but an apparently effective one: production continued with less interference from Moscow for a few months. But conditions were still difficult as winter turned to spring and spring to summer. Electricity was always in danger of being shut off, film stock was continually in short supply. And Eisenstein was pushing the actors to their limits. One after another of them fell ill, further delaying the shooting schedule.

At this juncture Eisenstein realized he had a strategic decision to make as to whether to release *Ivan the Terrible* as a whole. By early 1944 he had more footage than a two-part film could contain. He also realized that the middle sequences (what ultimately became Part II), were more explosive politically but also highly dramatic. He worried that Part I would seem unfinished if released alone *and* that Part II, lacking a triumphant ending, would seem too negative. He requested and received permission to transform the film into a trilogy and at that point his goal was to shoot all of Parts I and II and release them at the same time. Though he (and his cast and crew) were anxious to return the production to Moscow as soon as possible, Mosfilm remained in serious disarray even after the city had been secured, and he was freer from studio control in Alma Ata. Finally in July 1944 Eisenstein returned to Moscow where he completed editing Part I and, together with Prokofiev, finished the score and soundtrack.

In August and again in November 1944, Part I had preliminary official screenings before the Committee on Cinema Affairs, which imposed its first round of direct censorship. The committee required that Eisenstein cut the Prologue (Ivan's childhood) altogether, that he replace the titles at the beginning of the film with more patriotic ones, and that he counter the dark image of Ivan's guard, the *oprichniki*, with titles explaining their 'social and historical significance'.[20] On 7 December 1944, *Ivan the Terrible*, Part I, was screened in a 'corrected' version and on 31 December 1944 it was officially approved for release, by itself, without waiting for Part II to be completed. On 16 January 1945, *Ivan the Terrible*, Part I, was released in Moscow and within a few days it was being shown in other cities and on the front.

During the rest of 1945 Eisenstein worked hard to complete Part II. The major segment yet to be completed was the climax to Part II, 'The Feast of the *Oprichniki*'. Desperate to finish the film, he was disconsolate to discover that Prokofiev, who had yet to compose the score for these scenes, had become seriously ill and was forbidden to work. Another setback proved to be another windfall. The delay allowed Eisenstein to obtain some Agfacolor film stock, sent to Moscow by Soviet forces in occupied Germany. By the fall Prokofiev was well enough to finish the score and Eisenstein, intrigued by the possibilities of using the explosive dance scene to experiment in color, created one of the most dazzling and memorable segments of the entire film.

No one at the time realized the toll *Ivan* was taking on Eisenstein's health. He was traveling between Alma Ata where the shooting took place and Moscow where the sound and editing equipment was located. In Moscow, he was dividing his time between teaching and post-production, working almost around the clock. In December 1945, he submitted a finished version of Part II to the Mosfilm studio chiefs. On 2 February 1946, Eisenstein finished re-editing Part II and sent the completed film to the Committee on Cinema Affairs for approval.

The moment to release Part II could not have seemed more auspicious at the beginning of 1946, but appearances were deceptive. Part I had received enthusiastic reviews in prominent publications, which is to say that it had Stalin's blessing. Official favor continued to shine on *Ivan the Terrible*, or so it seemed, when Part I received a Stalin Prize in January 1946. But behind the scenes on the prize committee there had been deep opposition to awarding Eisenstein the Stalin Prize, and in the Kremlin cultural policy was undergoing a sharp, post-war about-face. The fate of *Ivan the Terrible* Part II would be decided while Eisenstein was too sick to play any role.

The very night that Eisenstein had finished Part II in February 1946, at a party celebrating the Stalin Prizes just recently announced, he suffered a heart attack from which he barely recovered. With Eisenstein in hospital, the Artistic Council screened Part II several days later, on 7 February. It was rewarded with intense criticism. But Part I had received a similar response from the same cast of characters, so there was hope that it might yet be approved for release. Ivan Bolshakov had managed to get Part I approved the previous year, but this time, exercising more caution, Bolshakov postponed the decision until a separate commission could be called to recommend revisions. We do not know whether his caution was based on his perception of the film's contents or on his sense of the shifting political winds. However, on 5 March 1946, the Central Committee of the Communist Party passed a resolution prohibiting release of *Ivan the Terrible* Part II, based on its 'ahistorical and inartistic' qualities.[21]

The wartime relaxation of state control over the arts was over and a renewed hardline approach to political conformity had begun. In August and September 1946, the criticism of *Ivan the Terrible* Part II was made public in two Central Committee resolutions. By this time Eisenstein was well enough to start a campaign to save his film. He wrote the obligatory article of 'self-criticism' in October. Later in the year Eisenstein and Nikolai Cherkasov, who was a member in good standing of the Communist Party, wrote to Stalin requesting a meeting to discuss the future of *Ivan* Part II. The meeting took place on 25 February 1947.[22] Although Eisenstein was given permission to remake Part II and complete Part III, he did not continue working on the film. He spent the rest of 1947 and the early part of 1948 writing a number of theoretical works, many of which included important analyses of *Ivan the Terrible*. He was at work on an article about the tragic theme in the film on the night of 10/11 February 1948, when he suffered another heart attack, this one fatal.

It would be another ten years after Eisenstein's death, and five years after Stalin's, that *Ivan the Terrible* Part II would be released.

Notes

1. 1923/1/554/62 [21 Jan. 41].
2. 1923/2/1167/15 [23 Aug. 1941].
3. 1923/2/1167/50 [23 Sept. 1941].
4. 1923/1/652/9–11 [5 Sept. 1942].
5. 1923/1/652/9 [5 Sept. 1942].

6. 1923/2/1749/3 [15 Sept. 1942].

7. 'The Heirs and Builders of World Culture', *ESW 3*, p. 182.

8. G. Mar'iamov, *Kremlevskii tsenzor: Stalin smotrit kino*, Moscow, 1992, p. 70.

9. *KZ* 38 (1998), pp. 173–246.

10. Jay Leyda, *Kino: A History of Russian and Soviet Film*, Princeton, NJ, 1983, pp. 365–82.

11. Cited in *Culture and Entertainment in Wartime Russia*, ed. Richard Stites, Bloomington, IN, 1995, p. 5.

12. Eisenstein's casting and the atmosphere on the set are discussed in *Eizenshtein v vospominaniiakh sovremennikov*, R. N. Iurenev (ed.), Moscow, 1974, pp. 315–413; M. Nazvanov, 'Prokliataia kartina: Pis'ma k Ol'ge Viklandt so s'emok fil'ma "Ivan Groznyi"', *Iskusstvo kino*, 1998, nos 1–2; L. M. Roshal', '"Ia uzhe ne mal'chik i na avantiuru ne poidu"' *KZ* 38 (1998), pp. 142–67; L. K. Kozlov, 'Eshche o "Kazuse Ranevskoi"', *KZ* 38 (1998), pp. 168–72; P. Kadochnikov, 'Stranitsy iz dnevnika aktera', *Prostor*, 1983, no. 2, pp. 145–64 and no. 3, pp. 168–90; N. Cherkasov, *Notes of a Soviet Actor*, New York, 1957; 'The People of One Film', *ESW 3*, pp. 305–16; 'PRKFV', *NFD*, pp. 149–66; Ia. L. Butovskii, *Andrei Moskvin. Kinooperator*, St Petersburg, 2000; R. Iurenev, *Sergei Eizenshtein: Zamysli. Fil'my. Metod*, vol. 2, Moscow, 1988, pp. 221–36.

13. R. Zakharov, *Zapiski baletmeistera*, Moscow, 1976, p. 310.

14. Serafima Birman, 'Neotpravlennoe pis'mo', *Eizenshtein v vospominaniiakh*, pp. 355–6.

15. Roshal', '"Ia uzhe ne mal'chik"', pp. 155–62; Kozlov, 'Eshche o "Kazuse Ranevskoi"', pp. 168–72.

16. 1923/2/1749/8.

17. Nazvanov, 'Prokhliataia kartina', p. 134.

18. Gleb Shandybin, 'V Alma-Ate', *Eizenshtein v vospominaniiakh*, p. 379.

19. A draft letter is in Eisenstein's archive but was probably not sent; see 1923/1/657/3–4; Iurenev, *Sergei Eizenshtein*, pp. 233–5; Roshal', '"Ia uzhe ne mal'chik"', pp. 162–3.

20. 1923/1/648/7; 1923/1/642/4–20.

21. RGASPI [Russian State Archive of Socio-political History], 17/116/249/101 [5 Mar. 1946], 'O vtoroi serii fil'ma "Ivan Groznyi"'.

22. 'Stalin, Molotov, and Zhdanov on *Ivan the Terrible* Part Two', *ESW 3*, pp. 299–304.

2. Analysis

The 'Unity of Opposites'

Eisenstein saw Tsar Ivan as a divided soul torn by contradictory impulses, a 'unity of opposites', and that concept structures the narrative and reigning aesthetic of *Ivan the Terrible*. Within scenes or even shots, ambivalence and contradiction rule. Objects, gestures, characters and ideas are represented multiple times by mirror opposites. Individual actions and events are open to numerous, conflicting interpretations. When Ivan punishes the boyars, we are cued to think that he is a visionary progressive ruler ridding his country of its genuine enemies, *and* an inhuman dictator arbitrarily destroying those who oppose him, *and* a tragically divided man. Do the boyars oppose Ivan because they are greedy and self-serving or because Ivan is violent, manipulative and power-hungry? When the Polish King Sigismund's court is depicted as a hothouse of sexual innuendo, with the king himself dressed as an 'effeminate' parody of a Renaissance prince, are we to admire the openness of the secular court and take seriously his claim that Poland stands as an outpost of civilization on the border of barbarian Russia, or should we see the absurdity and 'decadence' as condemnation of the Poles' arrogance, or should we laugh at the camp eroticism and homoeroticism? The crucial question is, of course, was Ivan's commitment to creating the Great Russian State a success or a failure? A victory or a tragedy? Heroically constructive or violently destructive? A justification or a condemnation of violence and one-man rule?

Eisenstein was equally, if not more, interested in the *ways* meaning can be generated by moving images, sound and color, and distorted by ruptured expectations, unprepared juxtapositions, infinite slightly altered repetitions, and strangeness. The tensions and conflicts in *Ivan the Terrible* are conveyed in part by means of seemingly endless repetitions, resonances and rhyming motifs. Visual imagery recurs frequently throughout the film, often in slightly altered forms or viewed from a slightly altered vantage point. On the surface these repetitions add to *Ivan*'s strangeness, but they also represent strategies for producing artistic meaning and overall effect according to Eisenstein's notions about the purpose of art.

The effect of constructing almost infinite lines of contradiction and repetition is, in itself, multiple and contradictory. Meaning is destabilized and elusive. We are forced to think hard while watching the film, an uncommon challenge in the Stalinist movie theater. At the same time we are encouraged to move beyond thinking altogether and allow our senses to guide our experience of the film. Eisenstein compels us to question our assumptions about power, personality, kinship and responsibility; about the lines between good and evil, progressive and reactionary, real and imaginary, and to suggest ways in which seeming contradictions overlap. And he asks us to question our ability to perceive similarities and differences. He challenges us to both participate in making meaning from the film and wonder about how meaning is made.

Ivan the Terrible does not raise, much less answer, a single set of questions or issues, but rather offers a field for experiment, exploration and speculation that encompasses division and contradiction, illusion and surprise. But this not to say that no coherent meaning emerges from the film or that Eisenstein's thinking was either cynical or relativistic. Mirroring, contradiction and ambiguity have specific political, psychological, aesthetic and philosophical purposes in *Ivan the Terrible*.

In *political* terms, power is real even if its uses are contested. The abuse of power leads to treason, violence and tragedy, no matter how well motivated. The ends do not justify the means. Political change is traumatic and cyclical, and can be entangled in motivations that are deeply personal and private.

In regard to human *psychology*, conflicts between people and, more important, *within* individuals, are natural and universal – and almost always tragic. The human psyche, for Eisenstein, was a knot of contradictory and unsatisfied impulses, which produce a desire for connection and unity. Identity is changeable and elusive: individuals slip back and forth between contradictory sides of their personalities. Those transitions can be traumatic, often accompanied by violence, and they are liberating, freeing people from the specificity of social roles and creating the possibility of transcendence.

The *aesthetic* structure of *Ivan the Terrible* is not an enclosed system but is meant to represent and express the almost infinite complexities of conflicts between and within people in such a way that each sensual experience combines to work as a single harmonious whole. Eisenstein's attempt to unify all the diverse constituent parts of a film (acting, speech, imagery, music, shot composition, editing, color, thought and feeling) was an extension of his earliest work on cinematic structure: montage. Eisenstein believed that creativity was rooted in deep structures of human thought and memory, both in individuals and cultures. He believed that we derive meaning from experience through the freeing up of memories lodged deep in our psyches. His study of literature, psychoanalysis, ethnography and myth provided him with a store of concepts for understanding thought and behavior as well as for conceptualizing artistic creativity. Religious – which is to say Orthodox Christian – thought and practice offered false trails to salvation. Transcendence, he believed, was to be found in art. The experience of great art, in which all the almost infinite elements harmonize, creates a whole greater than the sum of its parts, which he called *pathos*, and which takes us outside ourselves into a state of transcendence he called ecstasy – *ekstasis*. *Ivan the Terrible* was Eisenstein's last great laboratory for developing these ideas and provided the raw material for his late theoretical works.

The film's resulting complexity, in artistic and political terms, far surpassed that of any of Eisenstein's previous films. At times, there were moments when it threatened to overwhelm him. After three months of work on the screenplay, in April 1941, he wrote in his diary, ' ... these last few days, I have been tormented by the volume of *Ivan* – it is tempting just to write it out in a realist framework. But then the guilt of not sticking my neck out?!'[1]

Eisenstein's quest for unity and transcendence have been read as essentially totalitarian, but this is a misunderstanding of his politics as well as of his aesthetics and philosophy. The 'unity of opposites' was indeed a driving force for his thought and practice at this stage in his life, but it was a quest for a unity that he acknowledged to be ephemeral, a function of human longing and wishful thinking. Like Dostoevsky (a major influence on *Ivan*), who preached sainthood and salvation but is read today for his exploration of evil and the complexities of earthly life, Eisenstein's search for unity and transcendence produced a work of great complexity that defied unity in every frame. *Ivan the Terrible* continues to fascinate us for its profound sensitivity to tragic divisions, ambivalence, fragmentation, violence, doubts and for Ivan's profound desire for purpose and immortality.

Politics and History

The Great Russian State

Ivan the Terrible was one of several works of art that Stalin commissioned in a campaign to resurrect early Russian leaders and create Soviet pedigrees for them. The rehabilitation of Ivan IV was a pet project of Stalin's, who was seeking to justify the centralization of power in the hands of one all-powerful ruler and to rationalize the brutal terror he had unleashed on his own people. Ivan's reputation for ruthless terror and irrationality has always made the campaign seem eccentric, but for Stalin it probably seemed rational. The Soviet ruler took a distinctly Machiavellian view of his own role in Russian history and undoubtedly attributed the same to Ivan IV: establishing and protecting the central state (whether Russian or Communist), as well as his own position as head of that state, was more important than any individual lives that might be sacrificed in the process.[2]

For Soviet artists and audiences, however, Ivan IV was an odd choice for resurrection. He was, by all accounts, remembered as a bloodthirsty tyrant responsible for unleashing a campaign of terror against his own country, and a costly, unsuccessful war against Livonia, Russia's barrier to power in the west on the Baltic Sea. Ivan destroyed the country's elite and killed his own son and heir, plunging Russia into political and dynastic crisis. He divided the country into his own domain, the *oprichnina* and the domain of the ruling landowners, the *zemshchina*. The *oprichnina* has never been fully explained, but it has always been associated with the terrifying rule of Ivan's private army, the *oprichniki*, who dressed in black, rode black horses and decorated their saddles with dogs' or wolves' heads to frighten people. Ivan may also have been addicted to chemical pain-killers (scientists found an unusually high level of mercury in his remains), which in turn might have caused mental instability. On the other hand, he successfully began Russia's imperial expansion with victory over Kazan in 1552 and most historians now agree that the early part of his reign saw significant attempts at judicial and other beneficial state reforms. In the 1940s it was believed that Ivan was something of an intellectual; there was evidence suggesting that he had amassed a large library and that he wrote eloquently about, among other things, his conception of the proper exercise of autocratic power.[3]

Ivan the Terrible addresses three sixteenth-century political subjects: imperial expansion, state centralization and political violence. In the Stalinist context the element of sixteenth-century history with the greatest contemporary resonance was undoubtedly that connected with terror,

2. Ivan's Coronation.

tyranny and bloodshed (even when justified by national and imperial achievements). Contemporary state coercion and violence, which were almost inescapable, but never discussed in public, made Ivan a tricky subject for each of the historians and artists commandeered for the project. Eisenstein was fascinated by Ivan and his historical role, but he always viewed the tsar as a complex human being; a despot to be sure, but neither entirely monstrous, nor entirely 'progressive'. From the beginning, Eisenstein was intent on representing Ivan as a complicated character. In both published articles and private notes, Eisenstein wrote that he wanted to 'humanize' the tsar, to look beyond his one-sided reputation for brutality in order to understand what motivated him: 'Not to whitewash,' as he put it, 'but to explain.'[4] Eisenstein without doubt approved of Ivan's campaign to expand Russia's empire and centralize power in the hands of the tsar at the expense of the boyars, and he believed Ivan to have been an early theorist of Russian politics; so he was driven to understand how a talented and committed leader could become a brutal tyrant, a demagogue and a mass murderer. Early in his research he reported his desire to explain 'the process of becoming such a character as he became'.[5] That he knew from the beginning that he wanted to go even further, to offer a critique of violent despotism in general, can also be deduced from his production notes.

Eisenstein was well aware that a film with such a conception of Ivan would require a special strategy to evade the censors. 'The most effective way of hiding something is to put it on display,' he wrote.[6] Such 'Aesopian language' or 'hiding in plain view', is a time-honored Russian intellectual tradition. In *Ivan the Terrible* Eisenstein used several forms of subterfuge. He put 'on display' a surface narrative that was politically acceptable. Then he proceeded to undercut the surface narrative with editing, style and narrative diversions.

The surface narrative of *Ivan the Terrible* is the story that made the screenplay unobjectionable. Many viewers have accepted it as the primary narrative meaning of *Ivan the Terrible* in part because it corresponds to a common Socialist Realist plot. The hero sets off on a quest, the hero is challenged, the hero overcomes obstacles, the hero is triumphant. In this case, Ivan's goals are the establishment of the Great Russian State unified in the name of the people and the reclamation of Russia's ancient lands for imperial glory and security against external enemies. Ivan triumphs over disloyal friends and foreign enemies as well as his own internal doubts and personal isolation to persevere in his efforts to build the Great Russian State. The tsar repeatedly justifies brutal violence as necessary to protect the Great Cause against traitors and for the people. In the end, he defeats his enemies, establishes a unified state and expands the state's authority over new territories in the east by defeating Kazan, and in the west with victory over Livonia on the Baltic Sea.

Eisenstein undermines this acceptable narrative in several ways.

First, the actual plot departs significantly from the stated plot. Eisenstein plays to the expectations of his audience – that a film about the all-powerful ruler of the sixteenth century will reflect positively on both his own historical role and the role of the all-powerful ruler of the twentieth century – and then he defies those expectations.

The titles that introduce the film tell us exactly what we are to expect:

This film is about the man
Who in the XVIth century first united our country
About the Grand Prince of Muscovy
Who out of separate discordant and autonomous principalities
Created a mighty and unified state
About the Commander who spread the military glory of our motherland
    to the East and the West
About the ruler who, to achieve these great tasks, first took upon himself
The crown of Tsar of all Rus.

These opening lines frame our image of the tsar as bold, victorious, majestic, a Russian national hero. But the plot quickly takes a turn away from these themes. Instead of unification and in the midst of military glory we are riveted not by heroism and achievement but by conflict, accusations, illicit sexual play, treason, murder, conspiracy, terror and violent annihilation. As early as Part I, the state is not only *not* united, it is torn apart. And its tragedy is not due exclusively to the opposition of discordant, reactionary, selfish boyars, but to Ivan's own ruthless pursuit of power and his chosen methods for dealing with boyar resistance. The actual plot of *Ivan the Terrible* is anything *but* the story of the man who created a 'unified state', spread 'military glory' and achieved 'great tasks'.

Part I, which takes us up to the founding of Ivan's personal guard (the *oprichniki*) and private fiefdom (the *oprichnina*), and to the tsar's retreat from Moscow, shows Ivan to be a man who resolves to trick his people into submission if they do not choose him to rule over them and a man who creates his own army of inhuman sons without mothers or fathers to terrorize his political enemies. By Parts II and III, it has become the story of a man willing to destroy every living thing in his country in the name of an abstraction, the Great Russian State.

Second, the stated plot of the screenplay is undermined by the visual universe of the film. The heroic elements of the surface narrative were able to dominate perceptions of the written screenplay, precisely because it was presented textually, rather than visually. Themes connected with Ivan's conscience were less pronounced in the absence of the cathedral settings and religious objects that surround much of the action. The ubiquitous conspiracies and counter-conspiracies were less apparent to the official first readers of the script, without the repeated close-ups of sinister facial expressions and without the claustrophobia of the palace chambers where most of the action takes place. It is easier to believe in the goals of imperial power and state building before one has seen the bizarre movements and poses, the glaring and shifting eyes, the sharp turns of faces, the highly stylized and melodramatic mode of the acting. In other words, the surface narrative is powerfully challenged in a contest between words and images. The acceptable Socialist Realist plot unfolds within a film whose visual universe is composed of distortions, mirrors, historical falsifications, grotesque folk motifs, unsettling gender reversals, menacing icons, enormous, ubiquitous eyes and a myriad of other images which destabilize meaning and leave us wondering what to believe.[7]

Third, Eisenstein deflected attention from the dangerous elements of his film by publicly promoting a biographical interpretation that focused on Ivan's life as a 'tragedy in the Shakespearean mode'. According to this reading, Ivan's commitment to the Great Russian State cost him his wife, his friends, his allies, his kin, and isolated him from humanity altogether. From an exclusively Socialist Realist point of view, Ivan's personal sacrifice for the abstract ideal is a great and glorious feat. But Eisenstein meant us to read more into the film. Ivan's personal tragedy, his human isolation, is implicated in a wider web of events, which produced the national, historical tragedy as well. Ivan's isolation is marked as tragic personally *and* politically in all of Eisenstein's notes. By elevating a dehumanized, impersonal, utopian abstraction, the Great Russian State, above all personal ties of friendship and kinship, Ivan brings on both his own isolation *and* his country's destruction.

Throughout the two filmed parts and into the unfinished Part III, the orthodox surface narrative and its challenging mirror images contest one another with increasing visibility and intensity. The confrontation escalates steadily from beginning to end. In Part I, the acceptable surface just retains its primacy; elements of heroism and self-sacrifice in the name of the Great Russian State still have the power to contain (though not to justify) the elements of vengeance and violence. In Part II they do equal battle as the contest between worthy ends and brutal means comes to a climax. In Part III demagoguery, manipulation, violent annihilation, tragic loneliness and self-doubt negate the original appeal of the cause. Individual examples of disloyalty, treachery, deviousness and political maneuvering follow a similar trajectory through the three parts of the film. Consequences of treason, for example, become increasingly more serious and Ivan's strategies for dealing with his enemies become increasingly more convoluted and cruel.

This incremental process, by which the acceptable surface narrative is overwhelmed and destroyed, is set in motion by Eisenstein from the very beginning of his reading, thinking and sketching out of ideas in early 1941. There was no decisive break between Parts I and II, no change of horses midstream, as is commonly thought. The structures of meaning, the mirrors and contradictions, the surface and the underground, the intensification of repeated motifs and actions, were all in place at the outset and although Eisenstein continued to refine his conceptualization of the film throughout (and after) production, the historical and political critique of tyranny in Russian history was in place well before shooting began. As such, *Ivan* becomes a devastating critique of tyranny and a brilliant challenge to the conventions of Socialist Realism.

Throughout *Ivan the Terrible* there are references to recognizable Stalinist politics, policies and strategies. Part of the Soviet public in the 1940s might have been unaware of the brutality with which Stalin and the

Communist Party physically and psychologically tormented those the state considered to be Enemies of the People. But people like Eisenstein, whose friends and colleagues were caught up in the Terror, knew all too well the cat-and-mouse game Stalin liked to play with prominent intellectuals and Party members he had arrested. Eisenstein's personal experience in the dangerous 1930s were echoed in his representation of sixteenth-century Kremlin intrigues. He was personally acquainted with the politics of conspiracy and reprisal through his own narrow avoidance of arrest and through observing his friends and enemies. Both his mentor, Vsevolod Meyerhold, and his main tormentor, Boris Shumiatsky, fell prey to the Terror. Furthermore, Eisenstein's ability to survive was based on his mastery of the coded languages and masks of public discourse in the 1930s and his willingness to accommodate state mandates in order to keep making films. These compromises and their moral consequences also found their way into the stories of betrayal and survival, ends and means, doubts and determination that *Ivan the Terrible* tells.

Now let us turn to some representative scenes from each part of the film to see how Eisenstein constructed the political tragedy of *Ivan the Terrible*.

Ivan the Terrible, Part I

The surface narrative tells us that Ivan the Terrible was a Great Ruler who heroically overcame all obstacles and opposition in his effort to accomplish a Great Cause: the unification and expansion of the Great Russian State. Ivan's announcement at his Coronation that he will unify the Russian lands at the expense of the power of the boyars and the wealth of the Church, establishes two contradictory narrative paths. On the one hand, it initiates a classic Socialist Realist parable about a great hero, facing and overcoming terrible obstacles to achieve a worthy goal, for the good of his people. On the other hand, it shows Ivan as a fearful, manipulative tyrant who will carry out an unpopular policy, no matter what the cost to his people. The duality of the scene is symbolized in one of its final shots: Ivan glares sidewise into the camera, his face turned away, and the shadow of the imperial doubled-headed eagle is stamped on his cheek. Responses to the speech range from the indecision of Ivan's two best friends, Andrei Kurbsky and Fedor Kolychev, both of whom will soon betray him; the blind enthusiasm of several beatific-looking women, including Anastasia, soon to become Ivan's wife, eyeing Ivan with the same gaze offered up to Stalin in posters, paintings and films on display throughout the Soviet Union at that time; the conspiratorial murmurs among the foreign emissaries at the Coronation; and finally the fury of the old boyar and Church elites, who threaten to resist Ivan's attack on their power. These last include the Church leader Metropolitan Pimen, and boyar leaders Efrosinia Staritskaia and her son Vladimir who, though portrayed here as childlike, simple-minded and 'effeminate', is next in line for the throne.

The fate of the Great Russian State depends on Ivan's ability to retain the loyalty of his subjects. The major turning points in Part I come when Ivan tests his subjects and distinguishes the loyal from the disloyal.

In the rest of Part I (after the Coronation), Ivan is buffeted back and forth by alternating victories and defeats. The buffeting is paralleled by Ivan's alternating between decisive action and doubts. With each victory, Ivan solidifies his hold on autocratic power and with each defeat, Ivan reacts by choosing increasingly arbitrary and dehumanized retaliation. The surface narrative (and the introductory titles) state that the boyars' opposition was rooted in their selfish and reactionary attempts to hold on to power in contrast to Ivan's unselfish purpose to create a Great State for the good of the people. Though this 'positive' and 'progressive' Ivan remains throughout the film, his own battle to retain power will erode his moral high ground, revealing the dangers of autocratic power. Ivan's choices and reactions illustrate the ways in which power and the desire for power corrupt its holders and destroy them as individuals whether they are from the people or the elite and whether their goals are 'progressive' or 'reactionary'.

Part I ends with Ivan in characteristic contradiction: he appears to be dependent on the people's support for his rule and desolate in his loneliness, but in fact he returns to Moscow more powerful than ever after manipulating a massive show of popular support for his rule and establishing the power of the *oprichniki*, his own personal army of inhuman sons, over the old elite.[8]

Much of Part I is taken up by tests of loyalty, displays of disloyalty, and the tsar's responses to each. In fact, the fate of the Great Russian State project rests on Ivan's ability to retain the loyalty of his subjects. Until Anastasia's poisoning, he holds out hope that he can achieve his goal with the willing support of his people, including some of the boyars. The crisis at Anastasia's coffin, where disillusion threatens to undo him, instead leads him to embrace demagoguery, coercion and violence. But even before that point, he uses political manipulation both to test those around him and to coerce their support.

The Coronation displays his power, announces his plan to increase it, and tests the spectators' reactions to the plan. After the Coronation, the next three major sequences (the wedding, the popular revolt and the battle at Kazan) are apparent displays of power, challenged by acts of betrayal. The wedding shows Ivan expanding his power by marrying. But Anastasia's blind loyalty to Ivan is mirrored by the betrayal of Ivan's two best friends: Fedor Kolychev and Andrei Kurbsky. Kolychev refuses to serve a man whose policies he cannot support and he requests the tsar's permission to enter the priesthood. Kurbsky flirts openly with Anastasia and is tempted by Efrosinia's suggestion that he wants the throne for himself. Anastasia is torn by her own love for Kurbsky and her commitment to the tsar and his Great Cause. Efrosinia attacks on several fronts: she tempts Kurbsky, she conspires with the sinister Livonian Ambassador, and she incites the popular revolt that follows. But these are all still only hints of the challenges to come.

The first direct challenge to Ivan's rule comes from a 'dark mob' which floods into the palace, interrupting his wedding. The tsar easily subdues the rabble, but what makes this scene interesting are the various constructions of tsarist authority and the rhetoric that accompanies them. Under the leadership of Maliuta Skuratov, the crowd rushes to attack the tsar. Ivan pushes away his guards and Kurbsky intercepts Maliuta, who on seeing Ivan is suddenly overcome with awe: 'The Tsar!' Maliuta and the crowd behind him fall to their knees before the power embodied in the person of the tsar. Ivan's legitimacy (questioned elsewhere in the film) is confirmed in the eyes of the people – with one exception. Nikola, the Holy Fool, remains defiantly on his feet and accuses the tsar and his boyar relatives of using witchcraft to murder people, squeeze blood from their hearts, and destroy their homes.[9] Maliuta chimes in, with the claim that bewitched church bells were falling from their steeples.

Now Ivan steps up to the challenge. Ignoring the Holy Fool's claims to social justice, he turns the accusation of witchcraft into a joke – at Maliuta's expense. 'A head that believes in witchcraft is itself like a bell … empty!' Then he abruptly shifts direction (not for the last time) and turns the joke into a sinister threat. 'And a head can fall off all by itself? No, it has to be cut off.' Next, he equates tsarist authority with coercive violence. Those who disobey the tsar's orders 'will have their own heads cut off'. Then, the threat of violence is directed specifically at treasonous boyars and finally emerges as a general principle or rule: 'A tsar can only rule if he holds the reins. A state without reins is as uncontrollable as a horse without a bridle.' The crowd is in his hands by the time the scene is interrupted by the ambassador from Kazan, with the same single exception, the Holy Fool. Nikola's image has multiple resonances here. A defiant voice of the people, literature's Holy Fools often said what others were afraid to say. Nikola, however, is an odd-looking Holy Fool,

3. Fear and suspicion on Ivan's deathbed.

and almost totally out of place even in this bizarre version of the sixteenth-century Kremlin. His naked torso wrapped in heavy chains, this Holy Fool is none other than the stock image of a heroic proletarian from the revolutionary era: you have nothing to lose but your chains. He too is subdued by the tsar, but he goes down snarling in defiance, not laughing in complicity.

The surface narrative in this scene tells us that as Ivan asserts his authority over the people, he begins to win their allegiance. The way he accomplishes this shows the origins of his demagoguery. In a perfect parody of Stalin, Ivan asserts his authority by combining deceptive humor, capriciousness and threats of violence. First he wins the people over by pretending to join them in a joke at the expense of their comrade, mocking and scapegoating Maliuta, which traps the crowd in a kind of complicitous unity. Then, just when he has them in his grasp, he shifts tactics without warning to make it clear that if they do not voluntarily support him, he will use whatever force is necessary to maintain power. It is an infantilizing gesture along with a masterful display of demagogic tactics. And it works: individual young men admire the tsar's cunning, in humorously scapegoating Maliuta, even before he turns to threaten the boyars. It is easy to miss the full force of the tsar's threats of violence, because as he utters the words we are distracted by images of a different kind of boyar betrayal: Kurbsky's unsuccessful seduction of Anastasia. This is neither the first, nor the last, time Eisenstein will follow sinister humor with real threat.

On his deathbed, Ivan uses similar tactics to flush his enemies out of hiding. His near death gives them a false sense of security, forcing them to show their hands and bring their opposition out into the open. After provoking their displays of opposition, the genuinely distraught Ivan sets about ridding himself of his boyar enemies.

In the deathbed scene the surface narrative develops the threads of several obstacles the tsar must overcome: Kurbsky's double betrayal, the boyars' opposition, and Efrosinia's plot to place her son on the throne. Is Ivan really dying in this scene or manipulating his court with an elaborate pretense? Since Ivan knew about or suspected each case of disloyalty, the viewer has reason to believe that his illness was a ploy to test the boyars. Typically, the evidence points both ways and much in the scene seems intentionally mystifying. Eisenstein tells us that Ivan likes to be provocative; he enjoys 'daring' his opponents. He shares this trait with Efrosinia, identified by Eisenstein as 'Ivan in a skirt', but her provocations and tricks, unlike his, usually fail.[10] Though he is supposed to be dying, he looks surprisingly alert. Though he seems scared, he looks especially crafty when he peeks out from under the bible Pimen

4. Ivan's death hood.

5. The 'Eye of the State'.

has placed over his face. Whether we believe that he is truly ill or faking it, he manipulates his weakness in a reversal typical of this film, to transform himself and enhance his power.

Ivan's rebirth and transformation in this scene is central to the intersection of narratives in *Ivan*. Eisenstein plants markers of death and resurrection in every shot. He mimics a painting of the dead Christ in the placement of Ivan's body, in part to link Ivan to the martyrdom and resurrection of Christ and in part to convince us that Ivan will seem truly to die.[11] He lies motionless, face upturned, stone-dead and pale for several minutes of screen time. But the hood he is to wear after death is the visual opposite of a holy martyr's hood. Prominently marked with skull and crossbones, the death hood is even a photographic 'negative', white lines etched on black fabric. When Ivan finally rises, after the boyars have turned away from him, he seems to gather new, somewhat mysterious, decidedly sinister strength.

While dying, Ivan temporarily transfers his power and, in a sense, part of his body, to his deputy and seeing-eye dog, Maliuta Skuratov. Dressed up in his clean new eaglet outfit, he skulks along corridors and shadows of the palace, extending Ivan's reach and *especially* his sight. Surveillance is also carried out, or is felt to be carried out, by the enormous eyes of icons that spy down on the palace inhabitants, Kurbsky in particular. But the religious symbolism in these scenes is also curiously ambivalent. Kurbsky's betrayal occurs under the watchful eye of the state and the judgment of God, but whether the two are moral opposites or mirrored twins is unclear. Among other things, deep within the black iris of the icon is the barely discernible shadow of a skull. And while Ivan asserts that he has been resurrected by the power of the Holy Scripture, his image and acting suggest satanic power behind his revival. Is that the light of heaven or the flames of hell that Kurbsky sees when he peers into Ivan's bedchamber and realizes that the tsar is alive?

Ivan's demeanor is dramatically transformed from this point forward. Grief at Anastasia's death will only partly explain his embrace of violence. The deathbed scene implies that Ivan's mastery of manipulation, his power at a time of great weakness, and his miraculous resurrection is at least partly the devil's work. After the deathbed scene, Ivan displays only brief moments of ordinary human countenance, in Anastasia's presence, in Maliuta's before the finale of Part I, and later with Filipp in Part II. The rest of the time, Ivan wears a variety of masks.

Ivan's descent into terror and tyranny has often been characterized as 'madness', but there is nothing irrational or delusional about his behavior. Though he is often deceived and frequently ignores the evidence in plain view, Ivan never loses sight of his goal and always acts strategically. His behavior is eccentric and his demeanor strange, but he remains rational. His resort to mass murder cannot be dismissed as a failure of rational human faculties or abilities. If there is a demonic element to his behavior, it is a temptation that all human beings face, not the result of grief, depression or delusion, but from desire and will. This is not mental illness but moral weakness and political ambition. Ivan gives in to his darker desires for retaliation, not because he loses his mind but because he gives up his conscience.

To this point, Ivan's full force is not yet on display. He suspects but cannot bring himself to believe that those closest to him will betray him. Blinded by his own loyalty, he takes only half measures to protect himself and the Great Cause. He sends Kurbsky to Livonia to lead the imperial campaign in the west, a demotion presented as a promotion (except that Ivan pushes Kurbsky to his knees while claiming to offer him a raise). He arrests a few of the less prominent boyars and he demotes and banishes Pimen. Another provocation? Or a failure of will? Holy innocence or the devil's work? Either way his self-deception will kill his wife.

At work here is a curious set of contradictions within Ivan. He is far-sighted: visionary about his ultimate political goals but blind to the goings-on around him. He displays faith in Kurbsky and Kolychev long after they have betrayed him, and he refuses to believe that his aunt Efrosinia could be working against him. His faith in his friends and loyalty to his kin seem naïve and a little dim-witted, perhaps childlike. And those beliefs are contradicted, too, in hints of Ivan's cunning. He is pained by Kurbsky's ultimate treason, but he clearly suspected Kurbsky all along, both after Kazan and after the deathbed scene, when Ivan sends Kurbsky away from Moscow. And he suspects that Efrosinia poisoned his wife, long before he is willing to reveal his suspicions in public. Ivan's division between blindness to the evil near him and far-sightedness in imagining a glorious political future, prefigure his tragedy: his obliviousness about individual people dooms his abstract goals to fail.

The scene at Anastasia's coffin is the climax of Part I and a turning point in Ivan's evolving use of power.[12] The surface narrative here tells us that Ivan's grief over the death of his wife and lone supporter leaves him in despair; that despair leads him to doubt the validity of his sacred cause, the Great Russian State. But, just as despair threatens to destroy him, he finds the strength to continue. He chooses to seek support among the Russian people in order to continue the pursuit of the Great Russian State. Ivan's isolation in leading the Great Cause is personally tragic and his willingness to overcome obstacles is heroic. His final gesture at the head of his wife's coffin, arms flung in the air, is one of determination and triumph.

Ivan's determination is depicted in politically positive or personally tragic terms, but what is the actual outcome of his resurrection from debilitating grief? On the advice of Alexei Basmanov, he throws in his lot with the Russian people and vows to unify Russia in their name. The key transition here, from the boyars to the people, has a positive ring to it, but only until we look below the surface at the consequences of Ivan's decision. The instruments of Ivan's resolve are none other than the *oprichniki*. Synonymous with terror, mayhem and destruction, the historical *oprichniki* were responsible for widespread fear and violence, a fact well known to Russian audiences. In his notes Eisenstein describes the atmosphere among the *oprichniki* as one of profound disloyalty, where 'man is wolf to man'.[13] The satanic symbolism, first seen in Ivan's resurrection from death, is reiterated in this second resurrection. That Eisenstein intended us to link this resurrection from grief with Ivan's resurrection from death is cued by the repetition of an image of his head in the same position, horizontal, as in the deathbed scene. Ivan lays his head back on his wife's coffin echoing the Christ-like pose, and his beard forms a crucifix with the black candle behind it. At precisely this moment, when he reaches the nadir of grief and despair, he experiences a sudden surge of life-giving force: his grief becomes fury and his terrible vengeance is born.

But the *oprichniki* are not only the devil's army, they are the devil's family. When Basmanov recommends forming the *oprichniki*, he tells Ivan to 'choose men who will renounce everything, who will deny father and mother to serve only the tsar and the dictates of his will'. In other words, Ivan creates the *oprichniki* in his own image: alienated from all human and kinship ties, dedicated only to the political father, the tsar, and an abstraction, the Great Russian State. Basmanov goes so far as to *give up* his own son, Fedor, to Ivan. In this embrace of the abstract and renunciation of the familial, Ivan intimately and tragically entwines the personal and the political, the individual and the national.

This act, the founding moment of the *oprichniki*, is one of both supreme patriotism and cold sacrifice: Alexei's offering of his son is a double deception. His main goal, it turns out, is not to support the state for its own good, but to elevate his own family and guarantee its continuity through his son. He abdicates his role as father in order to increase the power of his family. Alexei gives Fedor to Ivan as the first son of the *oprichniki*, but he also enhances his clan's power by offering Fedor to

6. Alexei offers his son, Fedor, to Ivan.

Ivan as a replacement for Anastasia: he marries the Basmanov clan into
the dynasty. And the next time Ivan seeks support for his cause, he will
turn away from the dead Anastasia to ask Fedor what he should do.
When Fedor offers him the same simple loyalty that Anastasia had, Ivan
kisses his wife goodbye and welcomes his new children into the world.

Ivan further alienates himself from the world by establishing the
oprichniki as an exclusive 'brotherhood of iron', and vowing to trust no
one outside the brotherhood (not entirely trusting those inside either).
Although Basmanov has suggested it, Ivan's plan leaps fully formed from
his head. At this moment Ivan sees far more than his new lieutenants
from among the people, as is appropriate for the tsar. He understands
that he needs the whole of the Russian people to pledge support to him.
When Maliuta calls the people beggars and vagabonds, Ivan chastises
him: 'You are getting above yourself, cur. Do not presume to instruct the
tsar.'

This is a typical feint for Ivan, and it introduces the important theme
of political responsibility. Throughout the film, Ivan is careful not to
dirty his own hands with blood and he is not the only one to enable
murder without touching a weapon. Ivan initiates violence but has others
carry it out or, as in this case, he allows others to propose a plan, which
he then takes over. Ivan knows that he needs the support of the people,

and that he cannot entirely trust them to offer it, but that he cannot be seen to distrust the people. He also shows us both here and later that he will do whatever is necessary to ensure the people's support for the Great Russian State. If the people do not offer to support him freely, he intends to coerce them.[14]

Ivan caps the scene by discarding the idealism of the first enunciation of his Great Cause. The first time around, at the Coronation, he claimed the need to centralize power for the worthy goals of protecting the independence of the Russian lands and making a Great State. Now, in what Ivan tells us will be 'a new Coronation', the tsar seeks 'limitless power ... enabling him to relentlessly consummate the great task'. What justifies this 'limitless power' and 'relentless' dedication? If it was Anastasia's murder, then the motive is merely vengeance rather than a great historical mission. Eisenstein goes out of his way to emphasize not only Ivan's renewed commitment to his glorious cause, but a transition to pushing the cause beyond its original (and politically reasonable) limits.

The finale of Part I shows the entirety of society (peasants, clergy and boyars are clearly identifiable) coming to the tsar in supplication, falling into his trap. Ivan tested the Russian people by abdicating the throne; they have come to beg him to return and rule over them. With this act, the people abdicate their own authority in order to submit to the tsar for the purpose of supporting an abstraction, the Great Russian State. At the end of Part I, the dream of a unified, independent state (*samoderzhavie* in Russian) for the good of Russia and its people has been replaced with the reality of one-man rule, in which the ruler is isolated and his power centralized and unlimited (*edinoderzhavie*). He rules in the name of the people but he has created an instrument to secure and protect the tsar's power in case of opposition, the dark, wolfish and terrifying iron brotherhood of *oprichniki*.

The magnificent shot compositions of the finale emphasize the enormous power of the tsar and the minuscule insignificance of the people. Ivan has been speaking warmly with Maliuta about his fears and hopes as they wait impatiently together for the people to arrive, but when the people appear, Ivan drops his familiar persona and adopts a regal mask. He becomes a detached, impersonal, symbolic figure, an abstraction, the embodiment of the Great Russian State. The positive valence here is political: Ivan *is* the state, he embodies the people and the nation. But in human terms, he is inhuman, set apart, dehumanized and superhuman (in one note Eisenstein wrote, 'Nietzsche *was* about Ivan').[15] Eisenstein used repetition in the finale to powerful effect. In twenty-one separate shots Ivan is viewed from many different positions, with the tiny figures

7. Finale of Part I.

of the people snaking across the snow, obeying his every gesture. Ivan is truly awe-inspiring, an abstract, ritualized image of magnificence.

This scene is the last time we will see the Russian people as a whole. In Parts II and III they will be represented only in their darkest forms: the wolves and little devils of the *oprichniki*. In Part I we see the people in three scenes: as rebels storming the Kremlin, as soldiers in the Kazan campaign, and as supplicants in the finale at Alexandrova Sloboda. Although Ivan claims to rule in the name of the people and he derives his legitimacy from popular support, and although Eisenstein at times seems to take this justification quite seriously, the Russian people are portrayed in *Ivan the Terrible* as little more than instruments in the hands of the tsar. In the first instance, when the people exhibit passionate activism, they are easily manipulated and pacified. In the second instance, the people are introduced as soldiers at Kazan with an image that is passive in the extreme. We see a snaking line of soldiers (echoed in the finale), dropping coins on to a plate. After the battle the coins will be redistributed purely for the purpose of counting up the dead. The only commoners to behave actively and show initiative are Maliuta Skuratov and Alexei Basmanov, who will both become *oprichniki*. In the third instance, the people function even more passively than subdued rebels and battleground cannon fodder. They beg the tsar to rule over them, subordinating themselves to his rule. Ivan forces them to kneel and rise with little more than a twitch of his beard.

Eisenstein struggled to understand how the people could support this tsar historically, as he frequently wrote. His own genuine ambivalence is apparent in the contrast between his insistence on Ivan's popular base of support – 'He who is with the people is not alone' – and with images of the people as dominated, tested and tricked by the tsar.

There are several scenes in the screenplay that feature 'close-ups' of the people, in the form of a folkloric pair of fools known as Foma and Erema, depicted here as cannoniers. Eisenstein was repeatedly told by cinema officials that these two fools, who joke and sing and hit each other over the head, were not dignified enough to represent the Russian people. He agreed to cut the scenes and they do not appear in the finished film. But Eisenstein went ahead and shot two scenes with Foma and Erema anyway, despite all his earlier agreements. The scenes are genuinely funny and Foma and Erema are indeed undignified fools, so it is not surprising they did not make it to the final cut.[16] But they remind us that throughout production Eisenstein held on to his desire to portray the people as subordinated to the tsar and defiant to power. Laughter, Eisen-

8. Cannoniers Foma and Erema, deleted from Kazan episode.

stein tells, is 'the *one* thing that dares to deny the leading philosophy of its time'.[17]

Before moving on to Part II, a few words need to be said about two scenes Eisenstein shot for Part I but cut in response to criticism and censorship: the 'Oath of the *Oprichniki*' and the Prologue (Ivan's childhood). These two episodes introduced some of the darker and more damaging political themes of *Ivan the Terrible*. The Prologue offers a psychological explanation for Ivan's retaliation against the boyars and it links tsarist power closely to violence. The 'Oath' introduces us to the demonic atmosphere among the *oprichniki* by dramatizing the oath they pledged to the tsar. Eisenstein was willing to let the 'Oath' go, but he fought to keep the Prologue and was able to insert it as a flashback in Part II.

Footage of the 'Oath' has not been recovered, but the screenplay, a few extant frames and a series of remarkable drawings reveal a demonic, underground inversion of the light-filled cathedral of Ivan's first Coronation, while foreshadowing the Black Sabbath procession following Staritsky's murder at the end of Part II. Ivan is shown presiding over the birth of this dark brotherhood, each member of which pledged: 'To destroy the enemies of the state/To renounce my kin and my clan/To forget my father ... and my own mother/My true friend and my blood brother/FOR THE SAKE OF THE GREAT RUSSIAN STATE'.[18] Individual *oprichniki* were to be baptized in a ring, or crown of sharp knives.

Eisenstein considered this 'dark oath', which placed state interests above friend and kin and the political abstraction above the earthly and human, to be the source of all the 'sins' of the *oprichniki* and the catalyst for a chain of violence culminating in the murder of their leader, Alexei Basmanov, by his own son Fedor. Eisenstein makes it clear in his notes that *oprichnik* violence was not justified by the glorious founding of the Russian State, but rather deflected progressive political aims on to a path of degeneration and brutality.[19]

Critics on the Artistic Council of the Committee on Cinema Affairs responsible for releasing the film singled out this scene for its defamatory view of Ivan's policies. One powerful director on the council stated bluntly that, 'the Oath was absolutely unnecessary. The Oath lowered the figure of the ruler and his great significance.'[20] Pera Atasheva and others who saw the scene before it was deleted found it powerfully and deeply disturbing. Ivan's satanic leadership and unnatural fatherhood certainly would have been intensified by the inclusion of this underground baptism and dark Coronation, but deleting the scene did not erase these

9. The Oath of the *Oprichniki*.

plot elements entirely. The repetitive structure of the film endows Ivan with those characteristics elsewhere. And then because Eisenstein shot the 'Feast of the *Oprichniki*' in the summer of 1945, after he had consented to cut the 'Oath' from Part I (in December 1944), he was able to insert some of its crucial elements, namely the words to the oath itself, in that later scene. Emotional intensification through repetition and mirroring are lost, as is a closer identification of Ivan with the murderous 'iron brotherhood', but from the point of view of narrative, the information is there. Given the political sensitivity of the material and its threat to block the film's release, from Eisenstein's point of view, less was undoubtedly more.

The Prologue was a different story because it offered an explanation for Ivan's behavior to which the director was deeply attached. Eisenstein was committed to establishing a motive for Ivan's violence in the vengeance that grew out of his vulnerability as a child. The link between vulnerability and vengeance was central to Eisenstein's own identification with Ivan as well as key to understanding the links between the personal and the political. Though images from the Prologue will be repeated and inverted throughout *Ivan*, the later images lose not only intensity, but significance without their origins in the Prologue. Without the Prologue,

Ivan lacks a human dimension to lose, a tyrant to overthrow, a legitimacy to prove and a mother to avenge. The removal of these two important scenes deprived Part I of a considerable portion of its emotional and political impact. Deleting them had the ironic result of muting the critique of political tyranny but mystifying it at the same time. By the end of Part I, Ivan's behavior is no less demagogic or demonic, but it is less explicable and more confusing. Eisenstein secured the release of Part I and deflected attention from its darker themes and its political meanings, but it did not fundamentally alter the structure and purpose of the finished film.

Ivan the Terrible, Part II: The Boyar's Plot

In Part II, the orthodox surface narrative is increasingly challenged by the ominous elements coming to the surface by the end of Part I. On the surface, Part II consists of the tsar's successful struggle against his boyar and clerical opponents, now actively seeking to dethrone him. By the end, the boyars are utterly defeated and Ivan can turn, in Part III, to Russia's external enemies in the west and the glorious expansion of the empire. Tragically, the tsar is forced to act against his last friend, Fedor Kolychev, now known as the priest Filipp, and he is forced to destroy his relatives, the Staritskys, Efrosinia and Vladimir. In eliminating his disloyal friends and kin, Ivan sacrifices his own well-being for the good of the cause. He sacrifices his conscience and his humanity but the state remains. By the end of Part II Ivan has moved forward with his state-building project but the structure he erects is increasingly hollow.

The battle between Ivan and the boyars becomes more evenly balanced in Part II. The boyars' opposition seems more justified as Ivan and the *oprichniki* become increasingly vengeful, arbitrary, manipulative and violent. Along these lines, the conflicting components of Ivan's character seem more equally balanced as well. In Part I, the destructive and demonic were apparent but kept in check by the progressive. At the other extreme, in Part III, the destructive and demonic will dominate. Here in Part II, Ivan's progressive commitment to the state, his tragic isolation and his vengeful violence battle each other until the 'Feast of the *Oprichniki*' at the end, where Ivan takes on a decidedly satanic persona.

In Part II, Ivan's tragic and demonic impulses emerge in ways that emphasize deviousness, manipulation and indirection. This is important for several reasons, the chief political reason being that it obscures Ivan's personal responsibility for bloodshed. Ivan allows Maliuta to carry out the first round of executions. He ordered but did not participate in the arrest and presumed execution of Shuisky in the Prologue. His cold-blooded murder of Vladimir Staritsky is represented as a convoluted kind of self-defense, in which he has Vladimir killed by an assassin meant for the tsar. While on the surface, these scenes can deflect attention from Ivan's hand and absolve him of personal responsibility, in Eisenstein's thinking, they make him doubly culpable. Not only does he order the deaths, but because he does so 'passively', he both implicates others and avoids responsibility. His hands are clean but his conscience is soiled. Not coincidentally, this sort of devious indirection, by which the ruler rises above the actions of his henchman, was also one of Stalin's favored strategies and it echoes Ivan's clever manipulation of the rebellious crowd in Part I. The tsar can play the avuncular jokester (or the Friend of the Children or the Father of his Country) because he has other people to carry out his deadly serious threats. In yet another of the ruler's incarnations, Ivan's clean hands allow him to rise above the men around him, a Nietzschean superman, the embodiment of a principle.

By the end of Part II, deviousness is intensified as repetitions and reversals multiply, usually in more sinister form, exposing the dangers underlying specific images of state power depicted in Part I or drawing more people into the vortex of disorder and murder. To list only the most obvious examples, the Coronation is duplicated in Kurbsky's entrance to the Polish court, in Ivan's return to Moscow, and in his 'farcical' crowning of Vladimir Staritsky. The tsar's marriage to Anastasia has already been mirrored in his 'marriage' to Fedor Basmanov in the coffin scene and is repeated in Part II, in Kurbsky's 'marriage' pledge of fealty to Sigismund (which itself is mirrored in Ivan's caressing Maliuta before agreeing to execute the Kolychevs), and in the 'Feast of the *Oprichniki*' in the black swans, the drunken *oprichnik* leaders, and most obviously in Fedor's female mask and dress. The poisoning of Anastasia will reappear in the poisoning of Ivan's mother, in Fedor Basmanov's reenactment of the poisoning which forces Ivan to recognize that his own kin is against him and that he is both guilty and not guilty of poisoning Anastasia, and in Ivan's offer of the goblet first (empty) to Efrosinia and then (full) to Vladimir, filled with the drink that will be his undoing. Maliuta's change of heart (from rebel to loyal dog) will be echoed by Peter Volynets, who comes to assassinate the tsar but becomes a loyal servitor in Part III. Dual close-ups, cheek to cheek and nose to nose, will reiterate mother/child images of Ivan and his dying mother: Ivan and Filipp, Ivan and Fedor, Ivan and Maliuta, Ivan and Vladimir, and Efrosinia and Vladimir. Finally, the finale of Part II, the snaking procession of ersatz-monk *oprichniki* filing through the cathedral, recalls the snaking line of the whole population at the end of Part I.

In Part II Ivan's strategies for protecting himself (and the state) and punishing his enemies become more convoluted, immoral and cruel. In the final episodes, Ivan does not just protect himself from assassination, he manipulates a drunken, vulnerable child into taking the knife meant for him. He destroys the mother of that child, recalling (and avenging?) the murder of his own mother. He rewards rather than punishes the assassin Peter Volynets, and though Ivan is now the unchallenged master of his domain, he bows down to the lowly novice (echoing his bow to the people at the end of Part I and to Vladimir in the parody of Coronation) pretending to ignore the fact that the terrified Peter had come to murder him.

Escalating deviousness and cruelty are mirrored by escalating remorse. Fits of repentance and doubt are followed by renewed commitment to the Great Cause, but each time doubt is abandoned for determination, the cost of the Great Cause and the number of its victims grows higher.

In other words, Part II is less about subversive elements breaking through the surface narrative, than about open combat between conflicting uses of power. Ivan can no longer pretend, despite extraordinary efforts at self-delusion, that his friends and family support him. The first half of Part II revolves around Filipp's opposition and Ivan's devious retaliation against Filipp's family, the Kolychevs. The rest of Part II is taken up with an even more convoluted action against his aunt Efrosinia and his intricate reversal of her plot to assassinate him. While removing old enemies (friend and kin), Ivan develops new relationships with *oprichniki*, his new friends and family, who will also ultimately betray and isolate him. The only progress Ivan makes towards the Great Russian State in Part II is the increasingly cruel and dehumanizing removal of obstacles.

Part II opens with Kurbsky's pledge of loyalty at the court of King Sigismund, a scene that recalls both the Coronation and the wedding of Part I. The Polish court is a world of artifice and posturing; the king uses his power for preening vanity. The men in his court are dressed in absurdly effeminate versions of both western and Muscovite costume, the women wear heart-shaped headdresses and Kurbsky's breastplate is heart-shaped. Kurbsky's pledge of loyalty is a parody of homoerotic ritual (on his knees before the king, kissing first his sword, then his hand) and it recalls his diagonal, traitorous kiss of the cross in Part I. Kurbsky is also the object of the women's erotic desire. The stable center of the Muscovite court is absent here. It takes nothing more than a rumor of Ivan's return to Moscow for the king and his courtiers to scurry away. The chessboard floor reminds us of the chessboard Ivan sent to Elizabeth in his stateroom, and suggests that Ivan's power extends far beyond his own physical reach: he can manipulate the enemy court like pieces in a game.

Ivan establishes the major themes of Part II when he appears in the flesh on his return to Moscow from his abdication ploy. He divides Russia, in the name of uniting it (into *zemshchina* and *oprichnina*) and announces that he will stamp out treason. Just as he set out his policies at the beginning of Part I, Ivan's speech at the beginning of Part II can be seen as a new Coronation speech following the new Coronation he announced at the end of Part I. We see shots of his young servitors threateningly ranged along one wall with the old boyars in their cumbersome brocade caftans lined up along the opposite wall of the throne room. Finally, in a double blasphemous reversal, Ivan forces the boyars to their knees while raising his *oprichniki* to their feet, and claims God-like powers: ' ... as God created man in his own image, so I have created men in mine'. As if on cue, Filipp sweeps into the hall like an avenging angel, shouting, 'These plans come not from God ... but from the Devil!' In the surface narrative, Filipp's accusation can seem to be not much more than a religious cliché from the representative of Ivan's clerical opposition. However, the prevalence of demonic imagery already associated with Ivan, including the sacrilegious statement he has just uttered, show that Filipp was on to something. Throughout Part II and culminating in the 'Feast of the *Oprichniki*', Ivan will increasingly be associated with Satan and the *oprichniki* with little devils.

The personal and the political are entwined in this sequence of scenes in ways that take unexpected turns and have murderous consequences. When Filipp enters, Ivan addresses him as Fedor, his old friend and courtier, rather than as the enemy and priest he has become. Filipp resists Ivan's friendship, insisting on his new identity and oppositional stance. Ivan rejects Filipp's new identity and refuses to take Filipp's defection seriously. Of course, he *knows* that Filipp is no longer Fedor Kolychev, his lifelong friend and ally, but he wants his friend. Is this Ivan's characteristic blindness to those closest to him, is it pure disrespect for the Church, or a sign that friendship should supersede politics? Ivan seems surprised by his friend's cold rejection. In contrast, as soon as he sees Filipp, Ivan drops the official mask with which he had returned to Moscow to confront the boyars and adopts a genuine individual persona. We will see Ivan alternate between a cold, formal public mask and a warm, private authenticity on a few occasions, but for Filipp there is no division between personal feeling and political ideology. Once he rejects Ivan as ruler, he must reject the tsar's friendship. That does not, however, prevent him from using that friendship to try to save his family. Ivan begs for understanding but Filipp remains staunch. Filipp begs Ivan to spare his Kolychev relatives, but now Ivan remains staunch. As supplicant and master, they reverse hierarchical positions in spare, visually dramatic tableaux. Ivan begs for friendship on the basis of an impossible concept of friendship, hoping Filipp will overlook their political differences. Filipp begs for a political reversal based on an unrealistic understanding of politics.

Ivan pulls out all the stops in seeking Filipp's friendship, making a melodramatic appeal to his sympathy: 'You should really pity me … ' and takes us back to his childhood when he was tormented by boyars, to see why.

The political significance of the Prologue, inserted here in a slightly abridged form, lies in its justification for Ivan's conflict with the boyars and his desire for revenge against them. One of the reasons the Prologue works well here in the middle of Ivan's negotiations with Filipp is that it intensifies the linkage of the personal and the political, prefiguring themes that dominate Part II. It also takes place in the throne room of the Golden Palace, where Filipp and Ivan are standing, so it initiates a chain of repetitions in which scenes and relationships with similar dynamics occur, in particular relationships between characters that offer personal explanations for political action.

The Prologue opens with a shot of Ivan, age seven, alone in an empty, darkened antechamber: fearful, watchful and vulnerable. Suspense turns to nightmare when he hears a chilling (though stagy, melodramatic) scream and discovers that his mother, Elena Glinskaia, has been poisoned by boyars. She warns him against trusting the boyars, clutches him to her cheek, and moments later is taken away, arms dragging limply across the floor. A horrifying scene that was cut from the original Prologue follows, showing Glinskaia's alleged lover, Ivan Telepnev, running for his life through the dark passageways. Powerless himself, he begs the traumatized Ivan to save him, but the boyars pull him down into a pit of flaming torches while Ivan, mute and helpless, watches in horror.

After establishing Ivan's inability to save his family from the boyars, Eisenstein shows him unable to save his country from foreigners. A slightly older Ivan appears in the throne room during trade negotiations. He timidly mounts the throne and listens in, unable to intercede as Shuisky and Belsky, two powerful boyars (opposite in appearance, twins in self-interest), argue over which group of foreigners will control Russian trade. Political debate is a mockery, Ivan's power as ruler is a farce, and Russian leadership is a joke. Both Ivan and the country over which he rules are powerless and victimized by powerful forces around them.

10. First blood: Ivan watchful, threatened, vengeful, doubtful.

Back in the tsar's chamber Ivan leaps out of his victimhood. He emerges from silence, interrupts the boyars' pointless bickering and asserts Russia's need for independence. Shuisky and Belsky just laugh at him. Ivan reasserts his intention to make Russia independent of foreign control. The boyars just laugh harder. Here is another, slightly altered example of alternating humor and threat. Shuisky and Belsky are clownish in their arguing; their opposite appearance adds to the vaudeville comedy. But Shuisky lacks Ivan's cunning. He quits joking to challenge Ivan's legitimacy, his father's identity, and his mother's fidelity before attacking Ivan physically. The next shot of Ivan shows him disheveled and half undressed. Eisenstein deepens his justification for retaliation by depicting Ivan as physically ravaged and symbolically raped. The young tsar lashes back, making the final leap from victim to victimizer by ordering Shuisky's arrest: 'Seize him!' But this first taste of power scares Ivan: in a brilliant bit of direction, Eisenstein has him bark out the order, 'Seize him!' while stepping back and covering his own face. Ivan straightens his clothes and, addressing the camera, says for the first time, 'I will reign alone … I will be Tsar.'

When Ivan shouts 'Seize him!' the innocent boy casts off his innocence, tastes blood and experiences power for the first time. Individual power and Russia's independence are closely identified with, and only possible through, violence and retaliation. Ivan comes into his own as tsar by ordering a man arrested and executed. An important intensification occurs here: when Ivan makes the leap from victim to victimizer, he raises the level of violence and power that he wields over his former tormentors. When the hunted becomes the hunter, he unleashes a retaliation more brutal than the pain he suffered. Mysterious offstage poisonings will be replaced by the open execution of traitors. Individual attacks are about to give way to the mass murder of state enemies.

Eisenstein invested the Prologue with both autobiographical experience and with his understanding of human and cultural evolution. As a theorist, Eisenstein had a long-standing interest in the creative process, the origins of culture in primitive societies, and the way ancient myths and legends offered explanations for origins and transitions. He came to believe that transitions of all kinds – in individual development, between generations and in national histories – were traumatic and accompanied by violence. He believed that myths about such transitions represented actual, not metaphorical, experiences in human evolution and that individuals replicated those stages in their personal development. Eisenstein found confirmation for these hypotheses in his reading about Ivan and in his own life with his father.[21] He believed that adult tyranny and cruelty were defenses developed in reaction to childhood vulnerability and fears and that a profound shift occurs in the transition to adulthood, when individuals discover their own authority. Frightened or victimized children will mimic those they feared in order to displace them. If the passage to adulthood requires the ouster of a difficult or tyrannical parent, the transition will be traumatic and accompanied by violence. And that violence will bear within it the seeds of more violence. With the first act of defiance, the first taste of power is intoxicating and addictive. According to Eisenstein's notes, Ivan tastes 'first blood' in ordering Shuisky's arrest and again on viewing the corpses of the Kolychevs, the first executions that he orders as tsar. In both cases, 'first blood' intensifies his desire for vengeance and his willingness to shed blood to achieve it.[22]

Eisenstein intended us to see Ivan's motives as, on one hand, reactive, self-protective and just. His violence against Shuisky comes as a shock, but its deeper significance, its portent of more violence to come, is muted in part by the deletion of the terrifying murder of Telepnev. Close observation of Eric Pyriev's subtle characterization of the young tsar, however, brings out both sides of the future tsar's character. Pyriev conveys the watchful exterior and placid mask the young Ivan wore to disguise his fear and hatred of the boyars, and in the last shot, he captures the fires of hatred and ambition within. A shadow of the young tsar's innocence and appeal remains throughout, but his emergence as tsar is the emergence of a beast, the prey becoming the predator.

The connection between Ivan's cruelty and his fears is strengthened in the scenes that immediately follow the flashback. After claiming that the boyars called the tsar's vengeance upon themselves (they started it), his treatment of Filipp shows just how devious and dangerous he has become. He allows Maliuta, his faithful dog, to talk him into an act of supremely manipulative deceit that takes tsarist violence to a new level of cruelty. Ivan promises his old friend Filipp that he will be allowed to protect his Kolychev kin from the executioner, and then sees to it that they are beheaded before Filipp has the time to act. This crucial transition, from threats of violence to mass murder, is a logical progression from events immediately preceding, but is intensified by following directly from the flashback to his childhood.

Maliuta's motivations in this scene are also a tangle of political intrigue and personal jealousy. Ivan's most loyal supporter (who first appeared as his assassin) is fiercely protective of the tsar. In Part I he played Ivan's eyes by spying on his enemies, in Part II he will play the tsar's hands in carrying out his executions and delivering his sinister warnings. Maliuta not only serves Ivan faithfully and trusts him blindly (as faithfully and blindly as Anastasia had), but he loves Ivan. His love is unconditional, and unrequited. When Ivan detects passion on Maliuta's adoring, upturned face in this scene, he laughs, affectionately but dismissively, as if Maliuta were in fact a dog trying to reach up into the realm of human feeling. Maliuta suffers Ivan's rejection and the tsar's continual reminders of his lowly status with a smoldering jealousy. He is jealous of everyone else in Ivan's entourage. Eisenstein loved the idea that Ivan failed to appreciate the one person who cared most loyally for him. A crude, non-ideological creature, Maliuta kills for Ivan, stands in for Ivan, and represents the 'beast' in Ivan.[23]

Dismissing Maliuta to do his dirty work, Ivan is struck by a bolt of doubt. After the dynamic exchange between Filipp and Ivan and the affectionate, murderous exchange between Maliuta and Ivan, the tsar leaps up, rigid as a knife. He rises up in the frame, then the camera tracks up with him as he rises (echoing Ivan's rise at the end of the Prologue). With a hand covering one eye in a melodramatic gesture, he asks, 'By what right do you set yourself up as judge, Tsar Ivan?' His answer, or at least his self-justification, comes in the next scene, in Anastasia's bedchamber, where he is joined by another of his wife's surrogates, Fedor Basmanov. Fedor informs Ivan that the tsar's aunt, Efrosinia, left the goblet with the poison that Ivan gave to his wife with his own hands.

The moment of discovery in Anastasia's bedchamber is also complicated because Ivan must 'discover' its truth a second time before he accepts it. This is simultaneously what Eisenstein calls an 'atavistic' attachment to his own kin, which hinders him from retaliating against the Staritskys, and an excuse to proceed with his deadly assault on the boyars as a class. In other words, the discovery of the poisoned cup is and is not a justification for the executions that follow. Just as the Prologue was and was not a justification for those same executions.

Ivan's appearance at the site of the executions is one of the strangest in this strange film. He shuffles out, as if in a trance, bows, starts to cross himself, stops, and then glares at the corpses (or is he looking at his own burning soul?). Pointing offscreen to the bodies, he flings himself backwards, arching his back but straining and pointing forward, head up but eyes down, as if to embody contradiction. It is a moment of excruciating suspense and one of the central transitions in his life: will his first real taste of blood propel him further or end here? 'Too few,' he whispers, calling for more death. From this point forward, Ivan's animal instinct for vengeance will give him no rest.

The remainder of Part II will consist of his victory over two attempts to restrain him. First, Filipp tries to shame Ivan into repentance with a performance of *The Fiery Furnace*, an allegory about a tyrant and three innocent victims. But looking into this mirror and seeing himself as the wicked Babylonian King Nebuchadnezzar, Ivan not only does not repent, he embraces terror and, echoing the Prologue, asserts himself yet again: 'I will be what you call me: I *will* be terrible.'

The performance of *The Fiery Furnace*, with its other-worldly music, its dramatic confrontations, its 'Emperor's New Clothes' revelations and its demonic dénouement would make a remarkable scene in any context. Given the historical circumstances, Russia after the Great Terror and under Stalin, its contemporary allusions made it an act of almost incredible courage, or recklessness. The play, which was widely performed in Russian churches in Ivan's time and is depicted in several surviving frescos, derives from a story in the Book of Daniel that itself derives from the history of the Jews' Babylonian exile. After the tyrant Nebuchadnezzar had captured the city of Jerusalem and destroyed its Temple, he forcibly relocated much of the Jewish population to Babylon, a period of legendary anguish and despair for the Jewish people. In Daniel's version, three Jews are thrown into a fiery furnace and brutally executed for their refusal to worship idols, and not just any idols, but a huge golden statue of the king himself, who had declared himself to be like God. The story's contrast of innocence with cruelty, its marriage of the political and the moral, and its tyrant seeking Godhood offered Eisenstein a powerful set of parallels. This scene, more than any other, can be understood only in the context of Eisenstein's own time and it rings with questions relevant to Russia in the 1940s. With Eisenstein's affinity for mirroring and repetition, this scene is the most obvious reference to the world outside the movie theater and indeed the scene makes little sense in the orthodox surface narrative. The tsar's grim response to the public reminder of his murder of innocent people can hardly be seen as 'progressive', nor does it constitute the self-sacrifice at the heart of his personal tragedy. If anything, it echoes comments Stalin made to Eisenstein in their famous meeting in 1947, that Ivan was not terrible enough, that he 'should have been more decisive'.[24]

Filipp staged the play to humiliate the tsar but his plan backfired. In the original, the innocents who defied the all-powerful king are saved by an angel. In *Ivan the Terrible*, no angel appears. As one old man in the audience says pointedly, 'Those angels are extinct now' ('now' ambiguously indicating the sixteenth century and the twentieth) and it is Ivan who is resurrected ('I *will* be terrible').

There is more sinister laughter and a sharper contrast between humor and threat in this scene than in any other in *Ivan*. The evil tyrant's henchmen, the Chaldean guards who escort the boys to the furnace, are dressed and made up to resemble clowns (and boyars, with their patterned tunics and long beards). Boundaries of all kinds are blurred by these odd juxtapositions: between reality and spectacle, good and evil, heaven and earth, the past and present. In the most strangely menacing example, one Chaldean clown asks the other if it is indeed the tsar's order to burn the boys, if the boys had indeed disobeyed the tsar, and if they are to throw the boys into the furnace and begin to burn them for disobeying the tsar. With a series of twisted grimaces, the other affirms each question. This conversation is cross-cut, not with horrified faces of the boyar spectators, as might be expected, but instead, when the Chaldeans say that they will hurl the boys into the fire, we cut first to images copied from Ivan's Coronation of two women gazing with blind loyalty, and then cut to the little boy, laughing as the clowns talk about the vicious murder about to take place. In another mood switch, Ivan interrupts the deadly serious play, laughing loudly as he enters the cathedral.

Seeing him, the boys caucus and agree to sing the part most defiant of the tsar (and directed perhaps at the audience in the movie theater?): 'Why, shameless Chaldeans, do you serve this lawless tsar ... this devilish, blasphemous, despotic tsar?' That gets Ivan's attention. When he bows to receive Filipp's blessing, Filipp remains silent, and one of the boys glares straight at Ivan, singing, 'The earthly Lord will be humbled by the heavenly Lord.' Filipp not only refuses to bless the tsar, he calls Ivan a 'bloodthirsty beast'. To add insult to injury, the innocent child (ironically the only person in the room to think that the play was *only* a play but at the same time erasing the boundary between spectacle and reality, in case Soviet audiences missed the point the first time), spots Ivan and strips all pretense from the spectacle by recognizing him as 'the terrible, pagan tsar'. The adults around the boy cower in terror, except Vladimir (half-child himself), who laughs too until he realizes what the other adults already understand, that the child was right.

The scene ends with a shot that reverses the last shot of the Corona-tion: a close-up showing Ivan facing right and glancing left into the camera, shadowed now not by the double-headed eagle but almost entirely shadowed by his black robe and hood. Ivan has realized that Efrosinia is indeed his enemy, so he casts off his last family tie and accepts the young boy's truth: 'I *will* be terrible.'

The final scenes of Part II, 'The Feast of the *Oprichniki*', the assassina-tion of Vladimir Staritsky, and the procession of the *oprichniki* through the cathedral, show Ivan (and Eisenstein) at the height of their powers. Ivan towers over everyone around him, controlling each moment like a master puppeteer. The *oprichniki* dance, laugh and swirl about the room as if they were mere extensions of the tsar's demonic energy. He over-comes the most serious challenge to his rule without breaking sweat. And he makes sure that his powerful new lieutenants, Alexei Basmanov and Maliuta Skuratov, know their place as his 'slaves'. Ivan is all 'greatness and shrewdness' here, but in reaching so high he isolates himself still further from people and defies the human being within.

These final episodes are thickly layered with repeated motifs, mirror images, substitutions and reversals, yet while they allude to and even articulate contradictions, they point to Ivan's undiluted power and the clear-eyed cold-bloodedness with which he uses power here at the end of Part II. In the face of all this evidence of Ivan's demonic tyranny, it takes an effort to remember that Stalin found the Ivan of Part II to be insufficiently ruthless, indecisive and weak.[25]

The episode begins with an abrupt transition typical of *Ivan the Terrible*. The previous shot, Efrosinia slowly uncovering the goblet, ends with a double drum beat signaling her shock on discovering the goblet empty and introducing the frantically rising notes of the 'Dance of the *Oprichniki*'. After Efrosinia's slow-motion revelation, the viewer is stunned and enlivened by the sudden loud music, fast movement and color that characterize the wild, animal exhilaration of the dance, which is already

11. The dance is in full swing when we enter.

in motion when the camera catches it. The red-orange coloration and shimmering lighting make the frescos of the 'Forty Martyrs' on the wall and ceiling flicker as if lit by flames. Then it becomes clear that Eisenstein used his small supply of color film stock to plunge us into a chamber of hell. The *oprichniks*' costumes, simple tunics of gold, black or red, mimic and mock the grandeur and simplicity of the icons around them. The camerawork and editing of the dance emphasize its primitive energy, both seductive and fierce. The editing breaks up the dance numbers, never showing complete set-pieces, whose effect is simultaneously disorienting and mesmerizing. Eisenstein, never content with a single iteration of a movement, manages to make the dance seem even more menacing by interspersing it with ludicrous parodies of the dance hall and the folk dance. Gradually we realize that the dance is being invisibly directed by Ivan, through his agent, Fedor Basmanov, dressed in a gown and mask to resemble the dead Anastasia.

The 'Dance of the *Oprichniki*' takes on a number of layered meanings. It recalls the wedding of Part I but conspicuously draws our attention to its dark transformation of the original: black swans for white, a false bride in a mask, an all-male 'wedding', which also suggests (an interrupted) gang rape in the removal of Fedor's gown and mask by the heated, drunken men. This ersatz wedding is interrupted by an ersatz

Coronation (going backwards in time). The fiery dance also echoes the fiery furnace (the flames that devoured the three innocents) and it seems to prefigure the fiery destruction of the boyars, described in a song the men sing gleefully while laughing and flirting with Fedor.

Fedor plays multiple roles here too: he is the bride to Ivan's groom and, as both man and woman, the object of the *oprichniks'* desire. He plays a little devil in service to the master by keeping an eye on Ivan and directing the dancing according to his orders. We know Ivan is orchestrating every detail of the scene, first because the goblet he sent Efrosinia and Vladimir as an invitation to the feast was meant to show them that he suspected their plot, and second because we see Ivan giving Fedor instructions with his eyes.

Eisenstein's method reaches its apex here in the final episodes of Part II. All of his themes – political, aesthetic, psychological, philosophical – are represented by each character's multiple shifting representations, which come together as overlapping motifs rather than in some more realistic way. Fedor's multiple roles as Ivan's agent, wife, son and eyes surround the tsar as a reflection of his great and terrible, seductive and disturbing authority. The absence of the mother, Efrosinia, subjects her defenseless son Vladimir to that predatory power.

The geometry of this episode is complicated by cross-cutting between the dance and the drama unfolding at the other end of the banquet hall. The unrestrained dancing forms a counterpoint to the deliberate actions at the table, where Ivan toys with Vladimir and the older generation sits drunkenly and sullenly arguing. The three sets of action unfold within one another. The dancing is interrupted by Ivan's sly interrogation of Vladimir, which in turn is interrupted by the Basmanovs' two-fold jealousy of Vladimir. Fedor is jealous of the loving attention Vladimir receives, momentarily in the position of the tsar's beloved, and his father Alexei is jealous of the attention Vladimir receives momentarily in the position of the tsar's beloved son, a position he wants for his own son. These interruptions, the first under Ivan's control, the second in need of control, set up Ivan's attack on the Basmanovs in Part III.

Meanwhile the cat ensnares the mouse. In total control, Ivan feigns weakness and ignorance. Vladimir responds to Ivan's supplication, his drunken head on Ivan's knee, mimicking the previous scene in which Efrosinia persuaded him to participate in the plot. Just as Fedor is the son to two fathers (Ivan and his natural father Alexei), Vladimir is forced to choose between Ivan and his natural mother, Efrosinia. He makes a poor choice.

But first, Ivan's seduction of Vladimir is interrupted by Alexei Bas-

12. 'Aren't we bound by other blood, spilled blood?'

manov, whose usefulness is about to run out. Sweating and drunk, Alexei chastises Ivan for consorting with boyars, especially with a Staritsky. Here a number of interesting reversals take place, all of which bear striking resemblance to Communist Party politics of the preceding decades. Ivan has the power to utter statements that diverge significantly from reality, challenging our ability to distinguish truth from lies, and implicating anyone who believes either one. Agreeing with the tsar's lie makes one a lackey and a fool, but defending the truth against the tsar's word makes one another kind of fool.

Ivan tells Basmanov that it is not his job to advise the tsar, when in fact that had been his job: Ivan had taken his advice to create the *oprichniki*. Ivan tells Basmanov that it is not for him to raise his hand against the tsar's relatives, when in fact that was exactly the job Basmanov was hired to do. When Basmanov reminds him of this, Ivan denies it, saying that his own relatives are more precious than allies not related by blood: 'I don't hack down oaks to make room for wretched aspens,' though the destruction of the boyars and the elevation of the commoner *oprichniki* are exactly what Ivan had done. Ivan tells Basmanov that 'the ties of blood are sacred', when in fact Ivan has finally opened his eyes to his relatives' betrayal and is in the process of engineering their punishment for it. When Basmanov guardedly suggests that the ties of spilt blood bind them more closely than the blood of kinship, Ivan pushes him aside and says, 'You are not my kin. You are my slaves,' deflecting responsibility for the blood spilled and repudiating the oath.

This almost endless maze of reversals and contradictions is a repudiation of the politics that allowed Ivan to gain absolute, 'terrible' power. Now at the pinnacle of his power, Ivan sets out to renounce the policies that put him there and destroy the individuals who helped him get there. Ivan realizes that to hold power alone, his goal since the Coronation in Part I, he needs to destroy not only his original enemies, the boyars, but his new allies, the *oprichniki*. The allusion to the Bolshevik power struggles and the political purges of the 1920s and 1930s are unmistakable.

By now Ivan has realized that his new allies have turned out to be as bad as the old enemies. Alexei Basmanov wants power and wealth for his family more than he wants glory for the Russian state. Here, two political principles come into conflict. The old kin-based power of the boyar families is challenged by the new mass-based power of the *oprichniki* who renounced kinship ties and place their loyalty in the tsar himself. The boyars are ruthless in pursuit of power for themselves and their families. The *oprichniki* are ruthless in their protection of the tsar, but it turns out that the *oprichniki* seek the same kind of power the old elite enjoyed. In successfully supporting the tsar and his ideology, they undermine his cause. This repudiation of the sacred oath marks Alexei as an enemy of the state, but it also shows his essential humanity: he cares more for his natural son than for the abstract ideal of the state. Alexei is as divided as Ivan. Ivan's counterfeit concern for his 'son' Vladimir is reversed in Basmanov's genuine concern for his son's future. Both contradict stated vows to achieve their ends: Ivan's vow to destroy the greedy boyars and Basmanov's vow to place political loyalty above loyalty to his family. In both 'fathers', the oath and its repudiation prove a tragic flaw. Both reveal the corrosive morality of striving for power and the tragedy of autocratic, one-man rule.

These failings of the *oprichniki* were to be developed in Part III, when Ivan's revolution will begin to devour its own children, but they are prefigured here. In addition to the dialogue, the visual display of the episode with its intensely sensual elements brings a raw physicality into play. The explosion of color, music and motion draws attention to the instinctive, animal nature of vengeance, clan loyalties and the desire for power, which Eisenstein believed to be fundamental to human nature.

The repetitions and contradictions continue to multiply as the plot to kill Ivan unfolds and is thwarted. Vladimir, drunk now, 'blabs out' the plot and a parody of the Prologue, with its enthroned, powerless child, and the Coronation, with its transforming crowning, ensues. The duality Eisenstein strives for is never more clear than in this scene. Ivan is both victim (lonely child, lonely tsar, target of assassination) and victimizer (exploiting the child's helplessness, powerful tsar, engineer of assassination). A refiguring of the Coronation is apparent as Vladimir is crowned and discovers the thrill of power. Ivan's birth as tsar is reconfigured as Vladimir's death. The triangle formed by Kurbsky and Kolychev flanking Ivan at the Coronation is repeated here with Ivan and Fedor (at his most crocodilian and seductive) standing behind Vladimir's throne. Ivan (now the all-powerful tsar he forecast at the Coronation) bows down to the false tsar that he is sending to his death. Ivan is father to his people, but kills his son. He exchanges his tsar's garments for a monk's robe when he is at his most demonic. He covers both eyes when he has finally opened them.

Ivan lets Vladimir orchestrate his own demise. Actually this ploy is twice removed: Vladimir echoes Efrosinia saying 'Take the crown, take the collar.' Ivan answers Efrosinia through Vladimir (just as Efrosinia killed Anastasia through Ivan) and dresses Vladimir in the royal garments. Recalling both the ill-fitting garments the young Ivan wore on the throne *and* his undressing by his servants, Vladimir drunkenly allows himself to be dressed and crowned. The masquerade makes Vladimir both assassin and martyr, both powerless and tasting power. When Ivan bows down to Vladimir, he is genuinely surprised to discover that the boy who refused to understand why anyone would want the crown now finds it irresistible. 'He wants it!'

At precisely that point, the real tsar puts an end to the game: 'The farce is over,' he shouts, but the farce is not over, it is becoming deadly serious. 'Brothers, let us address ourselves to the Almighty,' Ivan urges, as he turns away from the sacred bond of blood, luring his young cousin to the death planned for himself. The *oprichniki*, now dressed in black monks' robes, with black candles, accompany Vladimir to his death. They slowly proceed into the cathedral, where color gives way to black-and-white. Vladimir sees death awaiting him (and momentarily turns blue with mortal fear), the monks push him forward through the passages and doorways, into the shadowy cathedral where finally Volynets stabs him. Ivan's last rival is finished off when Efrosinia reveals herself and discovers her tragic mistake.

Part II has three endings. First, the *oprichniki* drag Vladimir away and remove the crown from Efrosinia's paralyzed hands, while Ivan and the *oprichniki* masquerading as monks file past her grief-stricken form. Second, in a parody of Christian ritual, the *oprichnik*-monks file behind Ivan through the cathedral to the altar, reciting their 'dreadful oath' in the place of liturgy. Ivan sinks down, the *oprichniki* behind him drop to their knees, revealing the fresco of the devil being thrown into the flames of hell. The camera cuts back to Ivan, then to a close-up of Ivan, who looks up, covers both his eyes and mournfully answers the question he asked at the beginning of Part II, 'By what right do you set yourself up as judge, Tsar Ivan?' ambiguously intoning his answer: 'For the sake of the Great Russian State.' And third (in color), Ivan almost addresses the camera directly, and tells us that a tsar must punish the guilty. Now that he has defeated Russia's internal enemies he can take on the foreign forces who block Russia's power abroad.

In Part II Ivan achieves political supremacy, one-man rule, by allowing his enemies to kill each other off in a power struggle to dethrone him – just like Stalin. 'My hands are free,' Ivan exults at the end of Part II, and that is exactly the problem.

Ivan the Terrible, Part III

The surface narrative is stretched thin in Part III, which is to say in the published screenplay, a large number of drawings and notes, some stills, and a few minutes of film footage. Little is left of the progressive aims announced at the Coronation, or at least little that is credible. The themes of betrayal, remorse, political manipulation, destruction and death are far more prevalent and powerful than the establishment of Russian state power either at home or abroad. The stated goal of Part III is the campaign to reach the sea, but as much of Eisenstein's audience might have known, the actual war against Livonia was a national disaster not a victory and what takes place is not so much a battle against foreign enemies as against Russian traitors and defectors: Kurbsky, Pimen and the Basmanovs.

By Part III, Ivan's willful annihilation of the world around him (and within him, perhaps) leaves the country in ruins. Ivan pursues the 'military glory of our motherland/to the East and the West', but each action towards that goal has consequences so devastating as to undermine the progressive and positive qualities that goal had once possessed. Pskov and Novgorod rise up against Ivan; he defeats them by viciously annihilating every 'man, beast and bird'. He is forced to eliminate not only the treacherous boyars, but also the *oprichniki* who have proven equally treacherous. Even when Ivan reaches the sea, his victory is a hollow one. The sea obeys his command but the land behind him is devastated; all but one of his friends and servitors have betrayed him; and all are dead, including Maliuta, loyal dog to the end. Ivan's power is complete, but the

13. Ivan tests Staden with mockery and threats.

country he rules over is devoid of all life and meaning. He not only embodies the state figuratively, he is the only thing left of the Great Russian State. Independent 'self-rule', which has become 'one-man rule', has come to mean individual isolation and tragedy.

Each of Ivan's negative characteristics is highlighted in Part III: his suspicion, vengeance, manipulation and cruelty. A surviving fragment of one of the few scenes that Eisenstein managed to shoot indicates the ways in which Ivan's most sadistic and destructive instincts would come to the surface in Part III.[26] In an underground chamber, surrounded by his *oprichniki*, Ivan is perched at a writing table at exaggerated height, suggesting both his elevated power and recalling Anastasia's coffin. A knight enters. It is the German Heinrich Staden, who served the historical Ivan IV as an *oprichnik* and wrote a book about the *oprichniki*, which was one of Eisenstein's main sources for the film. For Eisenstein, the inhumanly cruel Staden represented the viciousness of both the sixteenth-century *oprichniki* and the twentieth-century Nazis. In this episode, Ivan neutralizes the spy Staden with the same alternating mockery and threats he had employed against the rebel mob who threatened him in Part I. Just as he manipulated the earlier crowd to laugh at their leader Maliuta, he toys with Staden here, making the *oprichniki* around him laugh. Pretending to catch him lying, he orders Staden seized and thrown into a dungeon, then rescinds the order, and then repeats it and rescinds it again. The *oprichniki* laugh on command and follow Ivan's changing orders without question. Fedor seems particularly avid to carry out the tsar's will, whispering threats in Staden's ear even after Ivan has released him. Arbitrary and sadistic, controlling the people at will, Ivan here is the very essence of absolute despotism and demagoguery.

This scene indicates that the devious cruelty Ivan displayed in thwarting the boyars and engineering Vladimir's murder would reach a new level. Each major episode in Part III repeats motifs from earlier scenes, to intensify their emotional impact, to multiply their meanings and to continue the trajectories begun earlier: Ivan's power grows and his use of violence becomes even more brutal and unsparing. In his approach to Novgorod, where Pimen and the boyars are plotting to rise up against the tsar, Ivan orders the annihilation of the entire population. His motivation is telling: *everyone* in the area must be killed, including the dogs and the birds, not because they are enemies, but because they *might be*. Ivan repeats three times that 'no one, neither man, beast nor bird' will be allowed to give away the tsar's battle plans and thwart his conquest. In revenge for the betrayal of a few, Ivan kills off the whole population. As he nears Novgorod, the vista is barren and and ravaged; dead bodies and burned-out ruins litter the landscape. Extravagant, unjustifiable violence raises a question with acute contemporary significance. Is extreme, preemptive destruction brutally rational or is it an act of irrational paranoia? As in earlier actions that have sometimes been seen as signs of Ivan's 'madness', there is no indication here of Ivan's being irrational or delusional. Incomprehensible cruelty is often labeled insane, but Eisenstein rejected such an understanding of Ivan. Extreme mass violence is terrifying and may be beyond our understanding, but it can be intentional and calculated. And this was no war against a foreign enemy or invader, but a campaign of domestic terror.

The massacre around Novgorod ultimately had the ability to stir Ivan's soul and, after crossing the terrain he had desolated, he suffers his worst attack of conscience yet. The climax of Part III is Ivan's repentance and confession before a huge fresco of the Last Judgment. Ivan, who suddenly appears to have aged a decade, lies stretched out on the floor in a corner before the fresco (a corner not unlike the one he occupies when he hears his mother's death scream). Ivan tries to exonerate himself: 'It's not wickedness. Not anger. Not cruelty. It's against sedition. For betraying the cause of the people.' Echoing the 'polyphony' of the coffin scene at the end of Part I, a monk reads out the thousands of dead, while the Basmanovs list the numbers of monasteries destroyed. Eisenstein's draw-

14. Ivan's repentance.

ings for this scene are truly agonizing. Ivan's emaciated frame leans on the wall, pleading with God (specifically represented as God the Father). His repentance seems profound and genuine. But the longed-for absolution is not forthcoming. 'You are silent … ?' Ivan writhes on the ground like the sinners on the wall abandoned to the flames by God's judgment.

Here in Part III, Ivan's vacillation between his superhuman persona and his fully human one becomes tragic conflict. Ivan can only create the Great Russian State because he has superhuman qualities and a cast of characters ready to act as his eyes, his hands and his executioners. But his conscience draws him back down to human stature again and again. Destruction and salvation are mirror opposites that collapse into one inseparable whole. But ultimately, Ivan can only be a 'tragic' figure because his motives were selfless and his goal was worthy one, and because he suffers remorse. Eisenstein throws even this justification into doubt with God's refusal to grant Ivan absolution.

Adding insult to injury, while Ivan moans on the chapel floor, the *oprichniki* carry out their own treachery. Right there in the shadows of the church, while monks continue to read out the names of Ivan's victims, and while Ivan bangs his head on the floor until blood flows into his eyes, Alexei Basmanov and Staden arrange to steal the ecclesiastical wealth from the Novgorod cathedral to keep for themselves. The circle of betrayal widens. Fedor discovers his father's duplicity and Ivan discovers his confessor's treachery: the monk Evstafi is in fact a Kolychev and a spy. Ivan has been abandoned by God, betrayed by Alexei, and now deceived by Evstafi. The tsar covers his eyes, orders Evstafi's arrest and one more time summons the will he needs. Resurrected with renewed diabolical strength, he uncovers his eyes and never looks back.

First, Alexei's greed proves that the revolution Ivan set in motion produced a ruling class no better than the one it overthrew. After discovering that the *oprichniki* were creating their own 'neo-feudal' order, with neo-feudal powers and wealth for their families, Ivan decides to rid himself of their services, but he does so in a particularly devious and sadistic way. At a banquet echoing the feast in Part II, Ivan publicly announces his discovery of treason among the *oprichniki*. Using only his eyes, Ivan chooses Fedor to behead his father, forcing him to choose between loyalty to his father and loyalty to the tsar. Amazingly, Fedor does not object. Ivan plays on Fedor's complicity, the guilt he already felt for not turning his father over to Ivan. This is exactly the sort of guilt the Communist Party relied upon in identifying people to carry out the crimes of the Great Terror. To hide their own minor sins of disloyalty, people committed more terrible deeds than they otherwise might have done. Ordinary people and Party members alike attacked their co-workers and neighbors to preclude inquiry into their own loyalty. Eisenstein himself was publicly attacked by film-makers eager to prove their loyalty in the 1930s.[27]

But compelling a son to kill his father is not terrible enough for Ivan, nor does it satisfy his need to subordinate the entire population to his will. After Fedor kills his father to prove his loyalty to the tsar, Ivan uses that murder to question Fedor's loyalty. And even though Fedor was willing to murder his own father out of loyalty to the tsar and abandoned his oath to the tsar only under the threat of death, Fedor returns to the banquet hall sensing that Ivan already knows of his infidelity. In a classic Stalinesque maneuver, Ivan reverses the oath to trap Fedor: 'You showed no pity to your own father, Fedor. How will you pity or defend me?' The situation Ivan constructs makes loyalty and treason interchangeable. Any and every choice is an act of betrayal. In a final coda of treachery Staden quickly stabs Fedor in an attempt to save his own neck, but Fedor provides one last service to the state by warning Ivan against Staden.

By killing off the Basmanovs, Ivan eliminates his last allies and abolishes all power other than his own. Only Maliuta is left, a faithful, unappreciated dog, and he dies in the final battle just before reaching the sea (coming up short even in the end). Kurbsky has another chance to show his cowardice before Ivan defeats all his enemies and finally reaches the sea.

15. Alone? The Finale of Part III.

Eisenstein sketched a large number of drawings for the last scene of *Ivan the Terrible*. Several depict the waves breaking at Ivan's command: the 'Apotheosis of Ivan'. Another shows a disconsolate Ivan walking dejectedly down the beach, battle smoke wafting up to the sky behind him, with an inscription that reads: 'Alone?' Ivan has never been so alone, so why the question mark?

Throughout the film, the surface narrative states that 'he who is with the people is never alone'. But the people are all dead or hiding. God is not speaking to Ivan. His dog, his brothers, his sons are all gone. Some of Eisenstein's notes suggest that Ivan is not alone because future Russian successes will secure the Baltic coast. Eisenstein originally planned to end *Ivan the Terrible* with an epilogue showing either Peter the Great conquering the Baltic, which he did accomplish more than a century later, or the explorer Ermak expanding Russia's grasp towards the Pacific, also a historical reality after Ivan's death.[28]

There are also hints in the screenplay that Ivan is not alone because he is already dead, along with everyone else. During the furious race to the sea, Ivan travels *backward* in time, mysteriously appearing a decade younger 'as he gallops past the flames'. Whatever remained of Ivan as a human being died in the battle for the sea. Characters in *Ivan the Terrible* repeatedly die, are reborn and resurrected, Ivan more than anyone else, so it seems possible that the Ivan on the beach is not alone because he has rejoined the rest of humanity if only in death, his final resurrection.

As we think back on the entire film, we have to wonder what was the fate of the Great Russian State? Eisenstein's notes repeatedly testify to his belief in Ivan's 'greatness' and the importance of his task for Russian history, but in the film, Ivan accomplishes the task in name only. Ivan's success and his glory never again match the height he attained in the light-filled cathedral under the golden rain at his Coronation. When he grasped the crown and placed it on his own head, he claimed power for the Russian state and embodied that power himself. That moment of dramatic transformation was his crowning achievement, his successful revolution. Everything afterwards was degeneration and survival.

Power

'In this picture [the basic theme] is *the theme of power*,' Eisenstein stated bluntly in a post-production analysis of *Ivan the Terrible*.[29] This is an important formulation and a critical one for understanding the film's characters as well as its politics. Whether or not power is the only theme of the film or even its most important narrative thread, Eisenstein's refusal to identify the film's theme with Ivan himself or with any one individual lets us avoid two simplistic interpretive projects that have derailed many a viewer. If *Ivan the Terrible* is about power rather than about *Ivan*, we can avoid a simplistic identification of Ivan with Stalin, or Ivan with Eisenstein or Eisenstein with Stalin or Ivan with anyone else. Placing a de-individualized concept of power at the center of attention allows us to focus on the question of how power was used at a given time in a given context. It also allows us to approach the question with the flexibility and subtlety Eisenstein intended: to see identity as an unstable, shifting entity, shaped by changing contexts and collecting together disparate, often contradictory elements. In other words, focusing on power turns our attention from any one historical figure to the uses of power, which opens up complex political and moral questions rather than setting blame in some fixed way on simplistically demonized individuals.

Second, if Ivan the historical individual is pushed off center stage, we can avoid the tedious task of identifying all of Eisenstein's historical 'mistakes'. Historical films, in general, say more about the worlds in which they are made than the ones they represent, a state of affairs that invariably confuses and irritates audiences, including professional critics and historians. There is no point, however, in chastising directors for bending history to their own artistic, political or other ends. Artists' legitimate goals do not need to include the historian's attachment to evidence. It is much more interesting to ask *how* Eisenstein used history than to bemoan the film's inevitable inaccuracies. We can examine the ways Eisenstein uses history to construct a context for understanding the uses of power in the past and the present.

Eisenstein's characterization of power as the central theme of the film also helps us understand his famous characterization of Ivan the Terrible, quoted above, 'not to whitewash, but to explain'.[30] Eisenstein's depiction of ruthless, dehumanizing power together with images of greatness and historical necessity do not automatically signify Eisenstein's approval of dictatorship or justification of mass murder. Though he sincerely identified with Ivan psychologically and he conveys the essential, underlying attraction of power, the film does not condone the tsar's revenge or ruthlessness, nor does it imply justification of Soviet power. There is not a single image of autocracy in this film that is simple or simply approving. Each glorious image of the tsar is challenged by ambiguity, mirroring and contradiction. Ivan retains our sympathy as an individual because Eisenstein unquestionably admired Ivan's goal, his ambition and his selflessness, his remorse, but the mass destruction carried out in the name of his abstract ideal – the Great Russian State – is repeatedly represented as destructive.

Still the question remains: in Eisenstein's conception of Russian history, does the end justify the means?

Eisenstein's answer is no. The end not only does not justify the means for Ivan, the means destroy him and undermine the end itself. Eisenstein tells us that Machiavelli cast a special shadow over his conceptualization of the sixteenth century, but that Ivan was unequivocally not Machiavellian. Eisenstein read *The Prince* shortly after accepting the commission to make a film about Ivan and he repeatedly tested his own conceptions of characters and their uses of power against his understanding of *The Prince*. Ivan *seems* Machiavellian, because he places the 'end' of state unity above his personal needs: the 'end' is more important than the 'means', but Eisenstein does not justify Ivan's behavior, and at the end the state is in ruins. Eisenstein applauds Ivan's efforts but makes it clear that he left Rus divided and devastated: the means doomed the end.[31]

Ivan's choices about using power are depicted in part by contrasting him with characters around him. Like the hub of a wheel (a common visual motif), Ivan is encircled by characters who represent alternate strategies. Ivan's centrality is portrayed visually and thematically: at times each character *is* Ivan and substitutes for Ivan. But at the same time, he stands above the other characters, each of whom represents some aspect of his character or some alternative 'means' to the 'end'.[32] In contrast to Ivan, Kurbsky and Efrosinia are Machiavellian. Kurbsky is Ivan's double; Efrosinia is 'Ivan in a skirt'.[33] Kurbsky shares Ivan's commitment to the Great Russian State, but he is vain and envious, weak and easily corrupted. He wants the throne (and the wife) for himself. Efrosinia also wants power for herself but her motives differ from Kurbsky's. She wants to maintain the feudal boyar order. Both will resort to any means to achieve their ends. Kurbsky betrays his friends and his country and Efrosinia destroys her own son. Eisenstein gives other characters some Machiavellian features, too. Filipp might seem selfless but opposes Ivan for the good of his family rather than the state. Like Ivan, Filipp is committed to abstractions rather than living people; he says twice that he will join the opposition to Ivan, not for his family but for the principle of family rule. Pimen, fanatically devoted to the Church, would also employ any means to destroy Ivan and protect the old feudal order: he is willing to sacrifice an ally (Filipp), because he is more useful as a martyr than alive. Alexei Basmanov seeks power, but uses it selfishly to create a neo-feudal order. Staden is pure selfishness and Maliuta is pure unselfishness, but he can only reflect the tsar's power, he cannot hope to hold it. Even the childlike Vladimir Staritsky discovers that he likes power when he finds himself sitting on the throne. Each character represents a variation on the theme of power and a counterpoint to Ivan's use of power. Eisenstein describes this structure as a fugue on the theme of power.[34]

Ivan is the sum of all these variations on a theme, he embodies the state as the central unity produced by the other characters' voices. Put another way, 'here Maliuta, Basmanov, Fedka, Kurbsky, Evstafi come together in polyphony of dramatic themes ... the tsar is the unifying image of the people of his epoch ... [in] the body of the tsar's power'.[35] As the embodiment of each of these alternatives, Ivan reflects both the dangers of great power and its equally important magnetism.

Ivan's external conflicts replicate his internal battle. He personifies a cruel, complex contradiction: his selflessness is both his salvation (enabling his remorse, underlying his heroism), and his damnation (placing him outside kinship and friendship). His selfless devotion to the cause is the source of Russia's power as a great modern state and the origin of his tragic pact with the devil, 'for the sake of the Great Russian State'.

The structural unity of the film is also deeply rooted in the attainment of power and its consequences. Eisenstein's conception of this link between structure and narrative has strong linguistic resonances in Russian that can be lost in translation. Structural and thematic unity [edinstvo] is

16. For the Great Russian State.

realized in the film's images of autocracy [*edinovlastie*] and isolation [*odinochestvo*]. The autocrat is all-powerful – *edinovlastie* means 'power concentrated in the hands of one' – but Ivan also suffers from isolation and loneliness, *odinochestvo*. The political concentration of power removes the ruler from ordinary human experience and, as Eisenstein put it, 'the first gives the theme of state power (progressive in the given historical stage) – the *political* theme of the film; the second gives the personal – *psychological* theme of the film. In this lies the compositional unity, personal and social, psychological and political.'[36] The unity of the personal and political in this comment has often been cited as evidence of the essentially tragic nature of the film embodied in Ivan's personal tragedy. Eisenstein links the personal/political unity here with what he calls, '*all three* decisive episodes'. The three 'decisive episodes' in Ivan's biography are not achievements on the path to building the Great Russian State, but rather Ivan's most cruel, politically motivated murders: the patricide/fratricides of Vladimir Staritsky, the Basmanovs father and son, and the confessor Evstafi. The murders are decisive moments because each one further seals Ivan's tragic and demonic fate and because, for Eisenstein, they reveal Ivan's essential nature as a man who would murder to stay in power.[37]

If Eisenstein did not conceive such tactics as Machiavellian, what sort of ruler was Ivan? Eisenstein rejected numerous standard interpretations as models for his Ivan as too dogmatic or simplistic. He also rejected the 'madmen' depicted, for example, in two famous paintings of the late nineteenth century by Ilya Repin and Viktor Vasnetsov. He drew bits and pieces of his portrait from the original documents and historical literature but he finally came across the essential image he was looking for in an article by the well-known nineteenth-century literary critic Vissarion Belinsky. Belinsky had also rejected numerous popular interpretations of Ivan IV for missing what he saw as the essential dualism of Ivan's character: 'We understand this madness, this animal bloodthirstiness, these unprecedented evil acts, this pride, and along with these, the scalding tears, the tormenting contrition, the humiliation in which all of Ivan's life manifested itself.'[38] Belinsky's image of a man whose divided nature was fused into a single organic being offered Eisenstein an image that coincided with his long-standing ideas about identity as a 'unity of opposites'. In political terms, Belinsky offered a framework for explaining why revolutions destroy themselves, how good ideas produce disastrous consequences and a good ruler can degenerate into a dictator. Not only does the end not justify the means, but there are not any final 'ends'. Autocrats rise and fall; states come and go.

Just as Ivan was a divided soul, there are two 'states' in Eisenstein's conception of the sixteenth century: the abstraction Ivan seeks to create and the actual government composed of living people. As an ideal, the abstraction is perfect, but empty or suprahuman. On the other hand, the real living entity is made up of people who are as divided, flawed and corruptible as Ivan, who fail to embody the perfection of the abstraction. The world they make is one of jealousy, treachery and betrayal, as power seduces even the purest heart. Ivan's attempt to sidestep human corruptibility by replacing it with a utopian abstraction failed to eradicate human weakness. The original idea was deeply flawed, like all utopian abstractions. Ivan's attempt to transcend the worst human instincts depended on the elimination of human needs for intimacy, connection and family.

People familiar with Eisenstein's mythic and allegorical versions of the past may be surprised to learn that he considered himself a pretty good historian. On numerous occasions, in public and private, he claimed that his portrait of Ivan was historically accurate. This was not as naïve as it sounds, but neither was it cynical political spin. Eisenstein never claimed to match historians' standards for accuracy and his *Ivan the Terrible* should in no way be mistaken for a historian's rendering of the past. But he concluded that he captured Ivan's essential identity, the cyclical history of Russian revolutionary change, and the links between the personal and the political that were central to his understanding of Russian history. And he did not believe that he was required to adhere to the details of Ivan's life or the historical period.

In this context, two points need to be mentioned. First, *Ivan the Terrible* was made during a period when professional historians were writing new histories of Ivan's reign designed specifically to justify Stalinist tyranny, terror and imperialism.[39] The basic points of Eisenstein's surface narrative accord with current trends in history writing, but all of these interpretations were driven by politics and ideology, not evidence. Second, it is important to remember that other Soviet historical films of the 1930s and 1940s also promiscuously invented history for ideological purposes. If some of Eisenstein's distortions seem arbitrary, they were almost entirely dictated by his interest in the film's most important themes. To cite just a few of many examples, both Maliuta Skuratov and Alexei Basmanov were actually boyars not commoners; there is no evidence that Vladimir Staritsky was mentally deficient or even unusual; the Metropolitan of the Orthodox Church, Makarii, did not oppose but supported Ivan's ascension to supreme rule; and of course events are compressed and reordered and much is left out. Eisenstein does not tell us exactly what principles guided his choices, but the often blatant and unnecessary distortions (such as Maliuta's class origins, which seem to have annoyed everyone) are suggestive. If professional historians disregarded historical facts for ideological and political reasons, he seems to be saying, why should a film-maker not be free to distort them for artistic reasons? In a world with scandalously little regard for ordinary scholarly standards, Eisenstein sought to represent what he saw as the essence of Ivan's character and his reign, but he felt free to represent them in the form he chose.

Ivan's state-building and imperial expansion campaigns, his struggle with powerful boyar clans, his creation of the *oprichnina*, the terrifying violence of the *oprichniki*, his childhood and the international context were all rooted in works of prominent historians.[40] Details of dress, iconography and ritual were carefully researched. Contemporaries unanimously attest to Eisenstein's attention to every detail, so we have to assume that his distortions were intentional as well. He must have had a variety of reasons for turning the disastrous Livonian wars into a victorious conquest, for example, a decision that, typically, has contradictory implications. Imperial expansion and the reclaiming of lands Russians considered to be theirs were important ingredients in the establishment of the modern Russian state and the Soviet empire. They were also a key feature of Stalinist history writing and during the Second

World War, the Soviet government promoted films with themes of expansion and conquest. The Soviet reoccupation of the Baltic states was to be celebrated, no matter when or how illegitimately it occurred. And Eisenstein may have been pleased that Riga, the city of his birth, was once again part of the country he lived in. But then in the screenplay, as already discussed, the conquest of the Baltic coast was an illusory victory for Russia. Not only did it come at the cost of moral and political bankruptcy, but, in real historical terms, that victory was a lie.

Eisenstein's support for state centralization also has to be seen in historical context. His justification for Ivan's state building can be understood in part as the wartime patriotism that captured everyone in Russia during the Second World War. But belief in Russia's need for a strong state predated the twentieth century and Eisenstein's views derived more from liberal, pre-revolutionary historians than from the ideological work of his contemporaries. He clearly took to heart the liberal historian Konstantin Kavelin's characterization of Ivan as the 'poet of the state idea' and his own article on Ivan as a Renaissance prince, with its attempt to find balance in the treatment of Ivan, could have come straight from Kavelin.[41] Early modern state building was at the heart of many of the works of the most respected nineteenth-century historians that Eisenstein studied in preparation for *Ivan*, many of whom are still read as standard sources today. It was, and is, widely believed that national survival and international power in early modern Europe depended on the successful establishment of a centralized state and a centrally controlled army. For Russia to join the European state system, it was necessary first to form a state.

Another staple of early modern history (at least as it was written prior to 1941) is the necessary displacement of feudal elites. State centralization in Western Europe entailed the subordination of local aristocrats to the power of the monarch. Eisenstein could conceive of Ivan's assault on the boyars as a progressive act based on reading liberal, socialist or even some quite conservative historians. Eisenstein also understood Ivan's destruction of boyar power as a revolutionary act and an example of class struggle. While he accepted liberal theories of state building, he repudiated certain strains of liberal individualism and remained a democratic socialist to the end of his life. He was never entirely satisfied with his representation of Ivan's popular support, but he believed that Ivan's attack on boyar power benefited the Russian people as well as the Russian state.

But while Eisenstein undoubtedly believed that it was necessary for Russia to have a strong central state, he also believed that the sixteenth century and the twentieth century needed to be judged differently. In the article he published in 1942 to stake out a public position for his film, he wrote that 'different historical periods require different approaches', and: 'Obscurantism and bloodthirstiness are two charges that will be leveled against anyone who, in the great age of the democratic freedoms of the twentieth century, uses the devices of a medieval feudal scoundrel dishonestly to seize power from his people, sending his own people into a new slavery, and makes his goal the submission and enslavement of his peaceable neighbors and other countries.'[42] The reference in this article was ostensibly Hitler, but no one could write publicly about Stalin in these terms and the parallel is obvious and accords with views Eisenstein expressed privately about Stalin and twentieth-century autocracy. What might be forgiven in Ivan was unacceptable in a twentieth-century ruler.

The difference between the sixteenth and the twentieth centuries takes us back to the theme of power. Here Eisenstein saw a significant difference which Stalin personally confirmed. Eisenstein very pointedly differentiates the dualism that characterizes Ivan's actions and the analogous bloodletting in his own time: 'In spite of the fact that Ivan is a progressive man of the sixteenth century, looking far ahead, he is still a man tied to ... the superstitions accompanying the religious fanaticism of the epoch ... And therefore Ivan's despair creates doubt – and the *theme of despair* grows into the *theme of doubt*: am I right in what I am doing?'[43] Ivan's medieval religious scruples made it possible for him to accept responsibility for the bloodshed he caused. Some viewers might see Ivan's ability to overcome his scruples and renew his dedication to violent state building as Eisenstein's justification for Stalin's crimes. But Stalin himself conformed to Eisenstein's more critical expectations by being thoroughly disgusted with Ivan's doubts. 'When Ivan the Terrible had someone executed, he would spend a long time in repentance and prayer. God was a hindrance to him in this respect. He should have been more decisive,' Stalin told Eisenstein when they met in 1947.[44] Ivan's dualism and his sixteenth-century superstitions compel him to see both the glory and the horror of Russian power and the tragedy in his role as ruler, a humanizing dualism that Stalin altogether lacked.

Stalin
Specific references to Stalin in Eisenstein's writing are rare, often ambiguous (his English, while fluent, lacked precision) and illuminating. But Eisenstein was a cautious man. He rarely recorded anything controversial in his letters or even his diaries. When he did venture to set down his thoughts on deeply personal or political issues in his notebooks, he invariably resorted to a foreign language.

There was never any doubt in Eisenstein's mind that his portrait of Ivan would be viewed as commentary on Stalin and he conceived it as such. The following diary entry, written in reference to his screenplay, gives us a rare clue:

> Alas! Much broader than one is allowed to think. Our art not outgrowing of a conviction of one's own subject but out of prescribed love or hatred. Up to a certain age – progressif. From there on ...? What lacks in the works of today is the inner conception of ideas (not so in 'Mexico' – *my* theme). 'John' [Ivan] – good – because personal *avant tout* – a mixture of one's self and the leading figure of our time.[45]

With his eccentric English, Eisenstein is saying that state supervision may have been progressive in the past but is harmful in the present, hampering artists in the development of their own ideas. The character of Ivan is 'good', because it contained a personal treatment of himself and a 'figure' who could only be Stalin.

References to Stalin in the film had to be veiled, but they are unmistakable all the same. First of all, Ivan treats his subordinates and subjects in ways that were characteristic of Stalin. Capricious and manipulative, Ivan uncannily replicates the specific ways Stalin toyed with his victims. In subduing the rebels in Part I, in maneuvering the boyars on his deathbed and the people in his retreat to Alexandrova Sloboda, Ivan mimics Stalin's combination of false warmth and genuine intimidation. The sadistic trickery in the murders of Vladimir Staritsky and both Basmanovs can be found in hundreds of descriptions of arrests, interrogations and executions. Ivan tests the Basmanovs' loyalty by trapping them into a denunciation and then using that betrayal to accuse them of disloyalty to him. Many of Stalin's most loyal subjects, including the Communist Party elite, showed their devotion to the Party by labeling innocent citizens Enemies of the People, only to be arrested later as untrustworthy themselves. Stalin was particularly sadistic to members of his own entourage. He followed Alexei Basmanov's prescription to 'surround yourself with new men who have sprung from the people and who owe you everything'. Then he arrested relatives of almost all of his closest advisors and made it impossible for them to protest.[46]

Stalin had followed Basmanov's next prescription as well: 'Choose men who will renounce everything, who will deny mother and father to serve only the tsar and the dictates of his will.' Russian revolutionaries since the nineteenth century prided themselves on their personal self-sacrifice and dedication. Their selfless idealism was widely admired and emulated, but after the Revolution, when the Soviet state began to require self-denial, its darker sides were revealed. Selflessness in the name of Dictatorship of the Proletariat soon led to the wholesale subordination of individual rights and of the private to the public. Under Stalin this tendency was represented by a widely publicized image of Soviet society as one big family, with Stalin in the role of Father to his People. Novels, films, plays, newsreels and newspapers harped on Stalin's paternalistic attributes, as well as lionizing a variety of heroic 'sons'. The 'iron brotherhood' of the *oprichniki*, their filial loyalty to Ivan in place of their own fathers, clearly mirrors this well-known element of Soviet political culture. Its public manifestations in the 1930s and 1940s were, of course, sunny, heroic and happy. The big family's all-inclusiveness, however, disguised a more sinister exclusiveness: whoever did not fit in to the big family was identified as alien and dangerous. Eisenstein's big family is similarly as exclusive as it was inclusive: no one outside the 'iron brother-hood' was to be trusted. On the inside, the big families of both the sixteenth and the twentieth centuries were cauldrons of intrigue, con-spiracy and murder. Eyes play multiple roles in this film, but at least one of those roles is a kind of secret police surveillance. As Ivan's eye, Maliuta is the perfect secret police chief, skulking around the palace to listen in on conversations and root out conspiracies.

Finally, *Ivan the Terrible* contains images that depict Stalinism as the degeneration of a once glorious Revolution. When Ivan fears that the people will not support him, he chooses to rule by terror, trickery and intimidation. He surrounds himself with new people, but the people Ivan promotes to serve him in place of the ousted boyars turn out to be no better than those they were called forth to destroy. Though Maliuta tells Alexei Basmanov that he has been infected with the boyars' sickness, they are both 'neo-feudal', by the end of Part II. The *oprichniki* turn out to be as attached to power and wealth as their predecessors and they create a new privileged elite, 'a new class' of *apparatchiki* as interested in their own survival as in supporting Ivan. It was no secret in Russia in the 1930s that the pre-revolutionary aristocracy was replaced by people who professed proletarian values but moved right into the palaces of the old nobility and took on the elite's exclusive privileges as well. But as Stalin and the Communist Party consolidated power, they found it necessary to destroy those who had challenged his power and then those who helped him destroy his rivals. Stalin understood that those who followed his orders out of political expediency, as Fedor Basmanov did Ivan's bidding, could easily turn and support the next powerful figure if their own survival were at stake. When Ivan discovers that his new supporters are feathering their own nests, his revolution devours its own children, in just as horrifying a manner as the Bolshevik Revolution ate its original supporters.

I am not suggesting that Stalin modeled his reign on Ivan's or that Eisenstein saw a direct correspondence between Stalin and Ivan. The point is that Eisenstein lived in a world that he thought resembled the world under Ivan. Both rulers destroyed revolutions that began with idealistic principles; both secured colonial empires and fought devastating wars; both unleashed inexplicable violence upon their own country and both enjoyed an incomprehensible level of popular adulation. Eisenstein understood it as his job to explore the reasons why. He used the world he read about to understand the world he knew from experience, and vice versa, he used his own world to try to understand Ivan and his.

Eisenstein's caution was not the only reason for hiding these Stalinist allusions relatively deep inside the narrative. Ambiguity and contradiction provide a remarkably apt metaphor for everyday life in Stalinist society. Endless spirals of mystification and confusing layers of repetition convey better than any realistic depiction what it was like to live in a world of illusion and double-speak, where official rhetoric was belied by everyday life (preceding by several years George Orwell's invention of dystopian Newspeak). Eisenstein's experience of Stalinist terror showed him first hand how brutal and unpredictable arbitrary power can be. *Ivan*'s multi-layered rendering of the role of the great ruler, in which the depths belie the surface, which itself is composed of contradictions and half-truths, captures precisely the dangers inherent in Stalinist society.

Finally, a film with no easy answers or clear moral positions was a genuine anomaly in Stalin's Russia. *Ivan*'s emphatic contrariness, its very strangeness, asserted the artist's right to ask hard questions instead of offering consoling solutions. This strategy produced the opposite of amoral relativism: it denied viewers a neutral vantage point and challenged them to reclaim their own authority to make meaning from observation and experience.

Autobiography and Psychology

Self-portrait
Autobiographical elements play an obvious role in Eisenstein's depiction of Ivan and they intersect in important ways with his theories of artistic and individual development. Eisenstein's research for *Ivan* prompted a host of associations for him. He found that he identified deeply with Ivan's experiences in childhood, which prodded him to examine his own history and eventually to write his memoirs. Ivan's personal life, from his

lonely childhood to his lonely death, was based on Eisenstein's reading of historical sources filtered through his understanding of his own psyche. He would often refer to *Ivan the Terrible* as his 'self-portrait'.[47]

The great drama in Eisenstein's private life was his difficult and unresolved relationship with his father and the absence of his mother, who left the two for the brighter lights (and more fun? more sex?) of St Petersburg when Eisenstein was eleven. He remained in his father's house until he was seventeen, when he moved to the capital to study civil engineering and lived briefly with his mother. Two years later, the Revolution began and Eisenstein was drafted into the city militia and later into the Red Army. His father, a staunch supporter of the old regime, 'a pillar of the Church and the autocracy',[48] emigrated during the Revolution and died soon after in Germany, precluding any possibility of softening, much less resolving Eisenstein's adolescent hostility towards him. His parents' rancorous relationship and subsequent divorce left deep scars. In his memoirs, Eisenstein examined his feelings about his parents in some depth and it seems clear that the unhappy family dynamics of his youth provided a model for his thinking about dialectics. Eisenstein was literally the product of a 'marriage of opposites'. The animosity between his parents, together with his mother's abandonment and his father's cold distance left him feeling alone, powerless and angry. Eventually he would seek to avenge his loneliness and powerlessness by rebelling against his father and giving Ivan powerful weapons for overthrowing the forces that had abandoned and victimized him. But, as he reported frequently in his autobiography and working notes, Eisenstein would never entirely eliminate the feelings that dominated his childhood: fear, obedience and loneliness. It is no accident that Ivan's confession takes place before an outsized fresco of God the Father.

Eisenstein experienced his father as a distant and unremitting tyrant, 'a typical bully about the house'.[49] He repeatedly identified his father with Ivan, twice catching himself writing 'father' in place of 'tsar', in his notes, and he explicitly linked his father's tyranny with Ivan's: 'my father was a beast, as Tsar Ivan is a beast'.[50] Eisenstein connected Ivan's (and his own) loneliness with his father's emotional withdrawal. When Eisenstein was working on *Ivan the Terrible*, he realized that 'Ivan's loneliness is connected with the favorite expression of *my* father (who was Terrible enough!): "*man is always alone*".'[51]

The pain the young Eisenstein felt over his inability to break through his father's silence or to stand up to his domineering authority would be replicated later in Eisenstein's relationship with Meyerhold, and to some extent with Stalin, and would find its way into his portrait of Ivan.

17. Eisenstein and his father.

Ivan's fear of predatory adults, his desire for retaliation, his own pursuit of power, and his loneliness all have roots in Eisenstein's early family life as well as in his recurring relationships with tyrannical men.[52]

Ivan's sexual ambiguity also has roots in the director's personal experience. A major source of sorrow and frustration in Eisenstein's life was his unsettled sexuality and his perennial lack of intimacy. He was attracted to both men and women at various points in his life, though direct evidence of sexual affairs is scant. He had a number of lifelong friends, including, especially, Pera Atasheva, the woman he married but never lived with, but he had no long lasting, intimate relationships with either men or women. His memoirs and diaries describe embarrassing moments when his sexual inexperience came to light. These include shame about his sexuality generally and anger at his father for failing to initiate Eisenstein into a world of manhood and for rejecting him when he confessed homosexual desires.[53] Eisenstein never wrote explicitly about homosexual experience, but many of his drawings from this period reveal what he could not record in words: desire, pleasure, pain and shame in connection with both same-sex and heterosexual acts.[54] Loneliness, vulnerability, depression and anger darken Eisenstein's private writings. Pleasure, humor, pride and affection are not absent, but they are at times overshadowed.

Important as it is, bisexuality was not the only autobiographical source of Ivan's tragic dualism. Eisenstein's sense of himself as a 'unity of opposites' was rooted in contradictions of many kinds: social, sexual, political. He was a child *and* a man, obedient *and* rebellious, kind *and* cruel, and so on. Eisenstein represented these conflicts in two different kinds of structures in the film: Ivan vacillates (between 'decisive action' and 'doubt', for example) and at a more complicated level, each of Ivan's characteristics contains both positive and negative valences. Ivan's 'progressive' commitment to the modern state, for example, could be achieved only through destruction and division. He rises above other people, but retains his human conscience. The questions this set of contradictions raises for understanding personal responsibility provide a good example of the layered structure Eisenstein employed.

Eisenstein invested Ivan and some of the people around him with a conflict between active and passive natures. Vladimir Staritsky is passive; he lets others take responsibility in his place. Filipp is passive until prodded into action by Pimen. Efrosinia is all aggression and Maliuta is especially active, he even takes on responsibility for Ivan's 'actions'. Yet each of these characters possesses at least a shred of the opposite. Vladimir takes part in the conspiracy despite his reluctance and then discovers he likes power. Filipp invokes religious commitments to stay out of the plot against Ivan, but when he gives in, he resorts to an abstraction that echoes Ivan's. Twice he repeats that he acts not for himself or for his family but for the boyars and the *principle* of boyar power. Efrosinia is quick to act, but she (like Ivan) enlists proxies to act for her; and her actions (unlike Ivan's) fail to achieve their end: the rebellion, the poisoning, the assassination all backfire. Maliuta is the only character who fully accepts responsibility for his actions, but his actions are all deadly.

Eisenstein admired people who were both enterprising and willing to take responsibility for the choices they made. Ivan both rises above this conflict and embodies both sides of it. He allows Maliuta to act on his behalf, which keeps his own hands clean, befitting a superhuman ruler, but as a human being, he evades the responsibility for his murderous acts. He kills Anastasia, but Efrosinia is responsible for that, he has the Kolychevs executed but Maliuta does the deed and takes the rap. He arranges for Vladimir's murder and pardons the murderer. In Part III he has a circle of people kill off his enemies: Fedor beheads Alexei, Staden stabs Fedor, and Maliuta strangles Filipp, all on his instructions. Each of these characters also acts on behalf of someone else. Maliuta acts on Ivan's behalf, Efrosinia on her son's, Vladimir for his mother, and Filipp for his family and the boyars. Only Kurbsky acts for himself and he has to go into exile as a result. They use sacrifice as a mask to disguise their own ambition and will. Only Ivan is truly selfless, though he acts on behalf of abstractions (the state, the people), but he is willing to sacrifice himself to achieve his end. Ivan's tragedy is not only rooted in the personal sacrifices he made in order to achieve his public goal. He rises above humanity only by sacrificing his own interior human qualities and his ties to the world of humanity.

Eisenstein played out his own internal contradictions in this multi-faceted portrait of Ivan and the people around him. Each character enacts a component of Ivan's driving desire for power and his shame over the compromises he was willing to make in order to achieve power. In his memoirs, Eisenstein relates a story that had had 'a profound effect' on him in childhood, which illuminates these conflicts. A young Persian hero, who felt he was called upon to do great things, was forced to abase himself and bide his time in order to accomplish great tasks later on in life. Eisenstein remembered finding the man's story 'utterly captivating: his unheard of self-control and sacrifice of everything, in-cluding his self-esteem, as he readied himself for the achievements to come'. Eisenstein adds that he had Ivan the Terrible abase himself similarly before the boyars when he feared he was dying. But now, he goes on to say: 'In my personal, too personal history I have had on several occasions to stoop to these levels of self-abasement. And in my personal, most personal, hidden personal life, this was perhaps rather too frequently, too hastily, and almost too willingly done – and also to no avail.'[55] That the self-abasement here is related to the politics of film-making is evident from the context. He wrote this passage on 15 August 1946, just when it became clear that all his efforts, all the compromises he had made to produce *Ivan the Terrible*, had failed.

> In the course of time I too was able to chop heads off as they stuck out of their fur coats; Ivan and I rolled in the dust before the gold-stitched hems but accepted this humiliation only in the cause of our most passion-ate longings ... For my part, of course, this chopping was metaphorical. And, more frequently, as I wielded the sword above someone's head, I would bring it crashing down on my own instead.[56]

His own sacrifice brought Eisenstein 'pain, and the bitterness of suffering, through which, as through the rings of hell, my personal, all too personal inner world moves from year to year'.[57]

Eisenstein not only explored dualism in the form of inner conflicts, he also had a long-standing interest in transitions between states or forms.[58] Despite repeated bouts of depression and defeat, Eisenstein believed in the possibility of redemption in life as well as the ability to escape from individual pain, through individual transformation. Art, in particular cinema, offered the possibility of an experience of rapturous trans-cendence when it was constructed in such a way as to produce a kind of communicative harmony. When everything 'works', when thought and feeling come together, the artwork achieves what he called *pathos* and the viewer is drawn into *ekstasis* (ecstasy), or 'standing outside oneself'. This transcendence has the potential to unite our conflicting halves and recover the part of us that is untainted by the pain and anxiety of life. For Eisenstein also believed that deep within each of us is something purely emotional, or what he called 'pre-logical'. Artists draw on the pre-logical in creating great works of art and spectators can experience a return to that state in viewing art.

Eisenstein did not, however, romanticize the pre-logical. He believed that the *ekstasis* was possible only by combining the pre-logical with the logical or, put another way, the primitive with the cultured, or feeling with thought. Eisenstein's reading in psychoanalysis persuaded him that much individual suffering was the result of the 'birth trauma'. According to Otto Rank, a pure emotional, pre-logical stage in human development exists before we are born, when still in the mother's womb, but it is traumatized at birth.[59] Art can re-create the pre-trauma, emotional state of the womb, but at a higher, more complex level. Some ambiguity exists in his thinking at this point. On the one hand, all art aspires to this transcendental state of ecstasy. But ecstasy itself is 'inert, lifeless', like life in the womb. In some of his writings, it is the transition itself that contains the ecstasy: the moment of 'illumination', the 'emergence', or as in dialectics, 'the moment when a unity is formed from opposites'.[60] He constructed *Ivan the Terrible* in such a way as to bring about the experience of *ekstasis* in its viewers, but he also created moments of ecstatic transition from one state to another throughout the film. Ivan dies and is resurrected more than once, Vladimir's death is also a pro- longed birth, pushed along a 'birth canal' by musical contractions and the inexorable *oprichniki*. All the characters squeeze themselves through small doorway openings to emerge transformed on the other side. Each of these transitions is accompanied by pain and contortion.

Eisenstein endowed Ivan with the whole gamut of human possibilities for regression to pre-birth innocence and progression beyond life's final transition to a superhuman synthesis of innocence and experience. He vacillates between states, as Eisenstein often felt himself to vacillate between his childlike fears and obedience, his rebellion against authority and emergence into a powerful adult. Ivan is frequently infantilized by loneliness and betrayal, as during his conversations with Anastasia, with Filipp and in his final confession. And he is empowered and energized by retaliation, as in the Prologue, at his Coronation, and at Anastasia's coffin. In Part III, Ivan's forward and backward movement is captured as well by his sudden aging (at the cathedral in Novgorod) and his growing younger in his ride to the sea (prefiguring his death).

This 'unity of opposites', the 'moment of illumination', and the creation of a new synthesis or unity, have an obvious sexual dimension and Eisenstein refers to the link between sexual and artistic ecstasy clearly if coyly in his memoirs. In life, as in art, moments of transition can be as painful as they are joyous. Sometimes when opposites attract, the result is not ecstasy but monstrosity and violence. A range of possibilities exists and the dialectical process is a dynamic, ongoing one. Not only does it encompass choices and randomness, alternatives and variety, but it mandates that rebirth is possible after death. Themes of death, trans- formation and resurrection recur in the political story analyzed previously; here their meaning expands to include Eisenstein's conception of human psychology.

The crossroads of Eisenstein's and Ivan's lives result in two kinds of transitions: the overthrow of domineering father figures, and the recurring cycles of birth, death and resurrection. Both are accompanied by violence, both offer possibilities for freedom and renewal but, in every case, Ivan chooses either death or satanic rebirth. Rebellions and transformations are represented with a variety of characteristic devices in *Ivan*. Mirrors and doubles suggest opposites which at times conflict and at other times collapse into one another as similarities. Triangles also abound in *Ivan the Terrible*, often representing dialectical processes in motion. Characters are paired or triangulated as if Eisenstein were experimenting with every possible combination of human relationship structures. In fact, beneath the surface of the political narrative, lies yet another story, the form-shifting family.

Family

Ivan the Terrible is replete with broken, dangerous, complicated, unnatural families, which appear, dissolve and reappear transfigured. These transitions and transformations are characteristically ambivalent in meaning, but like the narrative contradictions discussed earlier, they accumulate resonances over the course of the film. Eisenstein's cyclical family melodramas (like his cyclical theory of history) explore the ways families of all kinds shape individual lives and offer possibilities for pain and rebirth.

Ivan's childhood in the Prologue is rich with family symbolism, birth and death. The dark antechamber in which Ivan waits, curled up on the floor, is one of many womblike spaces, dark and tense with anticipation.[61] Ivan is finally 'born' himself, but only after all his parents have died. His father is nowhere to be seen, his dying mother is dragged to her death, paradoxically into the light, which is Eisenstein's metaphor for birth: the path into the light is the path back to the pre-logical *ekstasis*. Next to die is one of Ivan's illegitimate fathers, the man who is used to challenge Ivan's legitimacy (as child and ruler), Glinskaia's lover, Telepnev. The absence of Ivan's father and the deletion of the scene with Telepnev's murder turn Ivan's 'birth' into a kind of immaculate conception.

As an orphan, Ivan (and his country) are left in the care of unsuitable fathers, the greedy boyars. Ivan is reborn, this time as tsar, but only after he overthrows those ersatz fathers, taking revenge on those responsible for his mother's death. This birth, his transition from childhood to adulthood, is accompanied by violence: the overthrow of a tyrannical father, violence which marks Ivan and changes his fate. Eisenstein defends Ivan's violent retaliation against tyrannical father figures and for the progressive cause, but on another narrative level Eisenstein knows that Ivan's birth into adulthood is paired with death.

18. Young Ivan waits in the womb-like hallway.

For the rest of the film Ivan will try to re-create families. Deprived of his family in childhood, he continually experiments with new families, many of them either demonic or monstrous. He can never quite love the new ones and will eventually destroy them all.

At his Coronation, Ivan tries to construct a new type of family, the Great Russian State, with the tsar as father. In his memoirs, Eisenstein ties this act directly to his own life. The Coronation 'is precisely the emergence of an heir, freed from the ghost of his father, the prototype!' and he ties this emergence with his own 'Papa's overturned authority, with political revolution and with his own revolution in cinematic form'.[62] Ivan's emergence, his birth as tsar, is bathed in light, the unforgettable rays of light flooding into the cathedral.

At his wedding, Ivan establishes his own family, but the gain is typically tinged with ambivalence, loss and betrayal. Anastasia's function as Ivan's wife is limited. Before and after the wedding, Anastasia appears primarily in a political role (supporting the Great Cause) or a maternal role. Later on, she appears as the heir's mother and then just before she dies, as Ivan's ersatz mother. Ivan's only show of affection for her comes when she acts as his substitute mother, comforting him in his loneliness. She acquires sexual attributes only in her relationship with Kurbsky, which she virtuously, but barely, resists.

The wedding celebration itself is incomplete and interrupted, marred first by the loss of his friends Kurbsky and Kolychev, second by Anastasia's flirtation with Kurbsky. The wedding is then interrupted for good, before it is consummated, by the arrival of children: the Russian people. During the rebellion, Ivan teaches his children some manners, establishes his paternal authority and then sends his boys off to war, 'to Kazan!'

The Kazan battle scenes introduce a new dimension to Ivan's family. Until now, the family theme functioned vertically, involving primarily parents and children along generational lines. At Kazan, Ivan acquires some lateral relationships, men who function as brothers and lovers as well as children. He also acquires a second vertical family in the Basmanovs. At Kazan, Ivan argues with Kurbsky and adopts the man who will replace him, Maliuta Skuratov, who becomes the tsar's most loyal (and jealous) friend. Basmanov loves Ivan like a brother, though Ivan will remind him three times that they are not really brothers. Ivan also adopts Fedor Basmanov, but not yet. The Basmanovs represent a new kind of family, whose devotion places tsar and state above their own welfare, but this will prove to be a false, utopian hope, ultimately dashed. Each of these commoners will experience something like a rebirth in the Kazan scene. Maliuta's is particularly obvious, as he emerges from the underground and is called up the hill to Ivan.

Family disaster strikes next. The dying Ivan is forced to beg his enemies (or test his enemies) for their loyalty to his new state. A competing family, the Staritskys, come to prominence in this scene: the two mothers face off to secure the future for their vulnerable families. Efrosinia and Anastasia are mirror opposites. Anastasia is bathed in the light of virtue; she seems the quintessence of pure womanly, maternal love and fidelity, her baby a round-faced vision of innocent childhood. Efrosinia is barely a woman and carries none of the symbolic markers of motherhood. She is monstrous, unwomanly and deceptive; all ironically in the name of protecting her family's political power through the fortunes of her son. Vladimir is also childlike, but his innocence is called into question both by the political context of the scene and by the strangeness of the infantile, feminine qualities he possesses as a grown man.

Family disaster strikes again, this time leaving Ivan without his wife (who has never truly been his) and orphaned again. The scene of Anastasia's poisoning opens with a shot of a tapestry icon of Madonna and Child. In Anastasia's bedchamber Ivan, resting his head on Anastasia's chest in imitation of the icon, is torn between his child and adult personas. He learns (again) of the perfidy of his boyars and (again) announces his intention to assert power over them. Efrosinia realizes (again) that Ivan means to seize the boyars' power and she decides (again) to poison Anastasia, Ivan's only true (but not genuine) supporter. The knot tightens as Ivan realizes (again) that Kurbsky has betrayed him, Anastasia realizes that Kurbsky will never be hers and she realizes that Efrosinia is about to poison her. Efrosinia leaves the goblet with the poison for Ivan to hand it to Anastasia, who allows her husband/son to poison her. Ivan's (ersatz) mother is poisoned for the second time by the boyars, meaning he failed to heed his (real) mother's first warning. Is this recklessness, vengeance, blind trust or innocence? In this scene all the old families are torn apart to be resurrected in the next scene in a dark and monstrous form.

The climax of Part I is a key scene for the family theme. Ivan has been deprived of his natural family many times over and he is now truly alone. So he brings a new family into being. In a moment of ecstatic but monstrous transformation, he creates the *oprichniki*. Two opposites, Maliuta and Pimen, recite the reasons for Ivan's despair, but with opposite motives. Betrayal and abandonment plunge Ivan to the very depths of despair. The conflict between Pimen and Maliuta is mirrored in the battle for Ivan's soul: is he right or wrong to pursue the path he has chosen? At the moment he reaches the very deepest point of despair 'a sudden switch to the very opposite occurs'.[63] Despair gives way to determination. Ivan is reborn (again). He creates a new family, based on new (revolutionary) principles of family loyalty, which are public, political, inhuman, and diabolical. The scene at the coffin ends with Ivan standing triumphantly over Anastasia's coffin, his children entering the cathedral in a flood of light: a mass birth. The marriage of opposites at a moment of ecstasy produced a new generation of ersatz children, the *oprichniki*.

A chapter in Eisenstein's memoirs, which analyzes such dialectical rebirths, offers a model for understanding this particular birth. He describes his own unhappy parents as 'two people who were sick to death of each other', and his own birth as 'a grotesque caricature of the divine moment when man's threefold nature comes into one, at the very moment of the explosion of ecstasy'.[64] Ivan's creation of the *oprichniki* is another such 'grotesque caricature', which, along with Ivan's resurrection in a flash of ecstasy from the depths of despair, is produced by the two opposing voices of Pimen and Maliuta. The *oprichniki* are Ivan's children, but they are unnatural children, conceived in despair and violence, brought into being for the purpose of violence, willing to do violence to their own kin for the sake of the state.

The finale of Part I is a somber tableau of the new big family of the

Great Russian State. We see the reunion of the father with his people, but the triumph of unity is on the surface only, a purely public display, a mask. Ivan has another new family (still hidden), his 'iron brotherhood', on whom he depends. He needs a public display of popular fidelity in order to preserve the image of unity because the tsar has divided the Russian family in the name of uniting it.

In Parts II and III, family structures become increasingly problematic and convoluted. Births and resurrections multiply. Family ties become even more dangerous than in Part I. Ivan makes several moves towards an even greater patriarchal role, as a Nietzschean Superman, challenging even God's supremacy. His first move on returning to Moscow is to tell the boyars that he has created the *oprichniki* in his own image just as God created men in his.

In Part II, Ivan must deal with the opposition that comes from two different families: the family of his own kin, the Staritskys, and God's family in the form of the Orthodox Church. Ivan has a hard time relinquishing his attachment to his biological relatives. Even when the evidence is incontrovertible, he does everything he can to blind himself to the fact that his own aunt is plotting against him. When he finally does resolve to act against them, and destroys all his relatives, he gives up his last link with ordinary human morality. He becomes 'free' but it is a terrible freedom. In Part III, his independence from all human relations will enable him to sadistically twist family bonds among the Basmanovs and destroy them.

The Church functions as a counterweight to Ivan's other families. Filipp faces some of the same problems Ivan faces in trying to choose between his institutional and moral commitment to the Church and his biological and moral commitment to his family, the Kolychevs. His pledge to uphold God's law is challenged by his desire to protect and avenge his kin. Filipp is unusual in the film in his genuine commitment to Church teaching (mirroring Ivan in his supreme commitment to the state). In this context Filipp is Pimen's mirror opposite, flawed but selflessly devoted to his cause. Pimen is a devil in disguise and Evstafi, Ivan's personal confessor who figures in Part III, is a Kolychev in disguise. Pimen and Efrosinia (another devil in disguise, a 'devil in a skirt') tempt Filipp. He tries to persuade Ivan with reason and morality, but fails to protect his kin. Then he tries to convert Ivan with an allegory of violence, but fails to avenge the murder of his kin and is himself arrested. As Ivan's conscience, he is not very effective.

As traditional family structures fail in Parts II and III, they are replaced to some extent by Ivan's all-male family and we start to see sex play of all kinds *except* the heterosexual. Sexual inversions and reversals multiply and take on increasing meaning. Women all but disappear.

The women in this movie are comparatively insignificant to begin with. Elena Glinskaia, Ivan's mother, is killed off early, unable to protect little Ivan. Her function is positive only because she offers him the one genuinely affectionate gesture he receives in this film. But her tenderness is shadowed by terror and initiates a pattern of abandonment that Ivan will experience again and again. Anastasia is the one person who supports Ivan, but her support is impersonal, offered to Ivan as tsar, rather than as husband. And, anyway, she also gets killed off. Efrosinia is a woman, but is rarely depicted as one. Her 'masculine' features are contrasted with her son's 'effeminate' ones and they function as one of the major examples of role reversal in *Ivan*. The only moment in the film when Efrosinia takes on distinctly feminine, maternal, attributes is when she sings her lullaby to Vladimir. She throws off her black cloak and hood to reveal her white gown underneath, just before starting to sing. Her motherhood is tainted, too, by her willingness to force her son into a role for which he is unsuited and by her responsibility for his death. There are women boyars who function as reflections of blind faith in the tsar. And there are two servants who undress Ivan in the Prologue. Eisenstein also filmed a scene for the Prologue in which Ivan's nanny sings him a lullaby (she appears in the Coronation as well), but it was cut.

Let us remember that Eisenstein's mother abandoned him to the arctic emptiness of his father's house when he was a child. Though she remained in the Soviet Union and though he wrote hundreds of dutiful letters to her, Eisenstein never reestablished an affectionate relationship with her. In the film, Ivan eventually gives up trying to resurrect his mother and creates a band of lost boys instead.

Male relationships are hardly more satisfying than male–female ones. They are most often truncated, interrupted, substitutions, or predicated on violence and vengeance. Part II begins with a scene that depicts each of these: Kurbsky's pledge to the Polish King Sigismund. The king and his servitors are dressed in a parody of effeminacy: ostentatious lace-trimmed jackets and pantaloons, earrings, meticulously (and ridiculously) coiffed hair. Kurbsky, on his knees, offers Sigismund his sword in a gesture that can only seem sexual. They fetishize and kiss the sword. Before much more can happen, word arrives that Ivan is on the attack. The King and the court scatter, leaving Kurbsky on his knees, frustrated.

Other male relationships are equally fraught with frustration, interruption, conflict. Ivan's attempt to win back Filipp's love fails and leads towards the execution of Filipp's family. Ivan's loyal men do not fare much better. Maliuta loves Ivan but is beneath the tsar's consideration. Ivan keeps the Basmanovs by his side through much of Part II, but each move towards intimacy or understanding is followed by a move away.

Fedor follows Ivan to Anastasia's bedchamber (after Ivan has been rebuffed by Filipp). Here, his overlapping roles as son and bride to Ivan both evolve and Fedor acquires new closeness with Ivan. But Fedor tells Ivan something he does not want to know: that Ivan's aunt Efrosinia poisoned Anastasia and that Ivan gave her the cup with the poison with his own hands. Fedor hopes to impress and help Ivan, but has ensnared him in a web of difficult kinship ties (Ivan is, after all, a boyar himself), memories of his mother's poisoning (doubling his loneliness), and responsibilities for the death of both his loved ones (past) and his enemies (immediate future). Ivan entered his dead wife's room in an attempt to distance himself from the executions he had just ordered and possibly regretted. 'Let me not drink of this cup,' he says in an ambiguous statement of remorse. Fedor interrupts this thought and turns it around. 'You must drink from it. Even though some cups contain poison.' The consummation of Ivan and Fedor's 'marriage' on Anastasia's bed interrupts Ivan's attempt to seek both repentance and maternal comfort. Fedor binds himself to Ivan through forbidden knowledge and a chain of vengeance. Ivan interrupts Fedor's revelation and does not give himself entirely to the *oprichnik*, his adopted kinsman, because he is still tied to his own natural kin by what Eisenstein calls 'atavistic' feelings.[65]

The 'Feast of the *Oprichniki*' brings Fedor to the fore in a carnival of male camaraderie, flirtation and violence. Though the *oprichniki* depicted here are beautiful and their dance is captivating, it is impossible to escape the impression that Eisenstein's all-male world is a 'frightening and nasty' one.[66] The beautiful young men of the *oprichniki* dance like little devils and sing a song of murder. Their counterpoint to the inverted assassination plot reinforces the themes of treachery, vengeance and the brutal destruction of the boyars.

Typically for *Ivan the Terrible*, simplistic conclusions about sex roles are challenged by the proliferation of sex role images available in this and other scenes. Gendered identities are fluid in *Ivan the Terrible*. The *oprichniki*, Fedor in particular, are both attractive and deadly. The dance is shot in such a way as to prevent us seeing any single movement as a whole. The aesthetic effect of such fragmented movement is visually exciting, even spectacular, and it keeps us from attributing any fixed identity to the dancers. In addition, traditional markers of femininity and masculinity are associated with characters in a great variety of unconventional ways. Many characters carry bisexual markers of in-determinate gender. This has the (typically) paradoxical effect of both heightening the viewer's attention to sexuality and neutralizing actual sexual interactions. Eisenstein seems to endorse the idea of variety in sexual presentation and orientation, as well as transitions between various sexual identities, while at the same time ridiculing sexual pos-turing and play.

The homoeroticism and blurring of gender lines that pervade *Ivan the Terrible*, especially in Part II, have often been explained as Eisenstein's attempt to silence his own homosexual leanings. The 'marriage' to the *oprichnik* Fedor after the death of the innocent, loyal Anastasia, the gender reversal in the 'mannish' Efrosinia and 'effeminate' Vladimir; the absurdly costumed Polish court, and especially the combination of eroticism and violence in the 'Dance of the *Oprichniki*', are all coded primarily negative. But the proliferation of characters who blend genders in the dance also suggests the invocation of a transgendered or thoroughly bisexualized state. Rather than viewing the negative coding of homosexual features as Eisenstein's attempt at sublimation, it is possible to see here an attempt to escape from fixed sexual identities altogether. Neither male nor female, neither hetero- nor homosexual, the appeal of the dancing *oprichniki* is in the fluidity of their identities. Their violence defies conventional morality, but they also defy conventional gendered identity and assert their freedom from form.

Bisexual exchange has another role in Eisenstein's thinking. The inver-sion of male and female roles and the ritual cross-dressing that are highlighted here were central concepts in Eisenstein's thought about both simple and complex social role inversions. These ideas transcend both the political and the kinship narrative threads already discussed, as well as the most obvious clues to the significance of gender. Like Mikhail Bakhtin who is better known for it, Eisenstein was deeply interested in carnival as a site for freedom from everyday social roles. He saw inversions of ordinary roles as much more than a binary exchange between male and female or master and servant. He believed that cross-dressing or other exchanges of clothing were related to primitive ideas about superhuman deities who combined male and female in one body. He found ethno-graphic evidence of societies where exchanging clothes in marriage rituals was meant to evoke these androgynous beings and collapse or neutralize the differences between male and female. On the one hand, this collapsing of identities went along with Eisenstein's ideas (discussed above) about the ecstatic moment when the 'marriage of opposites' produced trans-cendence and brought something new into being. Unlike Bakhtin, Eisen-

19. Fedor as 'Ersatz Anastasia'.

stein was less interested in binary hierarchical inversions that occurred during carnival, though these attracted him too at times and are clearly represented in the carnival of the feast. But more interesting to him and more relevant to *Ivan the Terrible* is the emergence of a superhuman figure (as in Nietzsche) from the collapsing of sexual difference. Here in the feast, Eisenstein replicated the neutralizing of sexual difference through cross-dressing in a marriage ritual just at the moment when Ivan was casting off his last ties to ordinary human morality. Eisenstein emphasized that the emergent Superman can be either 'progressive and beneficial for mankind' or 'pathological'.[67] As Ivan tells us in the finale to Part II, his hands are free. He rises above the people around him, but then sinks down into his throne, with a look of demonic determination: progressive *and* pathological. Ivan rises above humanity but his conscience does not go with him and it keeps him anchored to the ground. Ivan is both the progressive Superman of Zarathustra and an ordinary mortal, who misses the intimacy he rejected and knows he has sinned.

Eisentein's cyclical families are not sites of happiness and self-fulfillment, but neither are they pure torture either. Even the nastiest families offer possibilities for rebirth and transformation.

Eisenstein invites us to analyze *Ivan the Terrible* through the personal experiences he describes in his published and unpublished writings. It

20. Ivan rises above the feast as a Superman.

would be a mistake, however, to read too much of *Ivan the Terrible* back into Eisenstein's own life. It does seem clear that he used the film to work through some of the moral, social and political threads of his biography. It is also clear that he was working in a context in which psychoanalysts and artists of various kinds saw early childhood and family relationships as models for understanding the social life of society as a whole.

Aesthetics and Visual Strategies

From montage to montage-image

Ivan the Terrible is an extraordinary-looking film. It contains such a wealth of images, motifs, symbols, musical cues, shot compositions and editing rhythms that one might be tempted to see the visual universe of the film as an end in itself. But nothing in Ivan is only artistically motivated. No gestures, images, objects or melodies are arbitrary or accidental. Repetition is neither ornamental nor neurotically compulsive, and images are not free-floating. All the images in *Ivan* are designed to suggest connections and to hint at significance, but such repetitions and linkages are always slightly skewed or altered. This 'almost, but not quite' set of connections makes discontinuity, distortion and disruption part of a system (rather than simply disrupting the system); a typical, paradoxical 'unity of opposites' in Eisenstein.[68] But while this structure complicates the process of deriving meaning from the film, it does not make meaning irrelevant or unattainable. *Ivan the Terrible* is an extraordinary film because of the dense ways in which Eisenstein has layered structure and narrative to draw viewers into his world, to awaken our curiosity, to engage us at our most primitive and intellectual together, at our most contradictory.

Eisenstein believed that a true work of art contains a tension between highly intellectual, conscious processes and emotional or 'pre-logical' response. Everything that makes *Ivan the Terrible* a haunting film (repetition, acting, camerawork and so on) provides a tool for mediating between the poles of that tension and ultimately collapsing them in order to create an experience of *ekstasis*. The ever-increasing volume of formal elements can seem overwhelming, but whether or not we can nail down the significance of every single gesture and object, we can appreciate the feeling of being plunged into a strange universe of mysterious excess, which Eisenstein used to draw the viewer into a dual process of thought and feeling. The thicket of associations seduces us into reading *Ivan the Terrible* at multiple levels, into marrying the logical with the pre-logical, into embracing the contradictory and experiencing *ekstasis*.

The primacy of the visual in *Ivan* draws attention to the unique ways films can tell stories. But the difficulty and elusiveness of the film's visual cues also remind us of the historical context in which *Ivan the Terrible* was made. The Soviet Union in the 1930s and 1940s was a society where public speech had become a tissue of elaborate lies and where public masks were worn to protect murderers as well as their victims. Soviet culture had become a combination of crude, simplistic narratives with unambiguous messages and surrealistic discourses that made no rational sense at all. Eisenstein's visual universe conveys the difficulties of making meaning in a world where ordinary markers of meaning are no longer reliable.

Ivan the Terrible is not a 'realistic' film. Its décor, costumes, sets, music and props thoroughly violate verisimilitude. Using a style known as 'expressionism', the physical setting does not convey a 'feel' for the real world of the sixteenth century or provide simple background to the action. Instead, the details of setting and structure take on importance of their own by insinuating themselves into the construction of character, event and meaning.[69] In realistic films, personality traits can be expressed by speech and body movement; in *Ivan the Terrible*, they are also signified by rhyming with symbols in wall frescos, objects on tables, shapes in the scenery or cues in the music, which surround characters and actions and identify traits. Unconventional speech and exaggerated body movements join unconventional architecture and exaggerated decoration and costumes to create *Ivan*'s characters and comment on their actions. Repetition and musical accompaniment create a network of associations that link characters and events and allow us to analyze or judge them. At a deeper level, such structural elements create an environment from which we can derive the film-maker's aesthetic and philosophic principles.

In *Ivan the Terrible* one of these central visual principles is strangeness itself. Strangeness serves a variety of purposes in the film. Eisenstein was one of many artists who called attention to the artificiality of art's representation of the world, by making the familiar seem strange. By 'making it strange' the artist invites us to look at the world with fresh eyes.[70] Obvious stylization also served the narrative strategy of 'hiding in plain sight'. Among other things, these strategies keep the viewer from imagining that *Ivan the Terrible* was purely about the past or purely about any one thing. *Ivan*'s visual strangeness immediately challenges us to look beyond the surface of the film for meaning lurking behind and beneath.

Images without obvious associations function like contradictory motivations did in shaping narrative: they raise questions that remain in the viewer's mind. Why does the camera linger on Ivan's discarded fur coat? Why does Vladimir grow a beard? Why are men dressed like women and vice versa? Why do so many characters draw attention to the act of dressing and undressing? Why do hands, feet, necks stretch out of their clothes? Why do people keep placing their faces unnaturally close to one another? Similar questions are raised by editing, shot composition, the musical accompaniment and the acting. Distortion, disorientation, exaggeration and repetition force the viewer to make connections that might otherwise seem arbitrary or contradictory. They taunt us with their difficulty, begging for meaning and resolution, but remaining at least partially unresolved. Nothing is what it seems, but if Eisenstein has piqued our curiosity at all, we want to solve the puzzles he poses and look behind his masks.

Analysis of visual effects is further complicated by the nature of the expressionistic style Eisenstein employs. Analysis of the acting, for example, cannot be entirely separated from a discussion of symbolic objects because certain gestures, like the stretching out of limbs or the movement of eyes, function much like repeated symbolic objects, like candles or cloaks or icons of resurrection. Eisenstein's use of space, for example, needs to be analyzed as a symbolic object *and* a formal device of shot composition and camerawork. Before turning to some examples of *Ivan*'s style and a discussion of the ways they reinforce the narrative issues discussed in previous chapters, a few introductory words are needed to place what follows in the context of Eisenstein's theory of film practice at this point in his career.

Ivan the Terrible looks so different from Eisenstein's previous films that many viewers took it to be a repudiation of his earlier revolutionary film practice, known as 'montage'. Eisenstein, however, saw *Ivan* as a continuation of the 'montage' style he had developed in *The Battleship Potemkin*. Put simply, the purpose of montage had been to juxtapose images through dynamic, jarring editing in order to produce a certain effect on the viewer. While working on *Ivan*, Eisenstein was surprised to discover that he had constructed it along similar, though much more complex, lines. In both films, what he called 'polyphony', or multiple voices and images, are brought together to produce a single heightened apprehensive experience for the viewer.

In silent film, the absence of sound and color limited the possibilities for dynamic film-making and drawing in the viewer. Eisenstein developed dynamic, rhythmic editing and the startling juxtaposition of individual shots in order to maximize the impact of cinema's purely visual effects. The addition of sound and later color offered the film-maker new dimensions for affecting the viewer. In *Ivan the Terrible*, Eisenstein uses the same techniques of dynamic editing and jarring visual juxtapositions, but now he expands the field to include combinations of images with sound, *within the shot*. He also juxtaposes startling images, not only from shot to shot as in earlier montage practice, but from episode to episode. Among his earliest notes are ideas about using 'jagged rhythms' between shots and episodes to replicate the indistinct memories of childhood.[71]

He also developed two practices used extensively in *Ivan*, known as 'vertical montage', and the 'montage image'. In vertical montage, music and image functioned the way single shots had functioned in earlier montage. Music and image are synchronized, but without coinciding perfectly, to achieve a more complex fusion of disjunctured elements. The montage image refers to the way Eisenstein constructed complex characters and ideas through the juxtaposition of visual and conceptual fragments. As Yuri Tsivian puts it, 'Ivan's true identity cannot be taken in at a glance. What matters is not so much what we see at any given time but our response to contradictory clues; a dynamic effect that Eisenstein used to call *montazhnyi obraz*, or montage image, in order to distinguish it from imagery that is merely visual.'[72]

Eisenstein's later writings show how every single element in a film plays a role in the montage effect. When all these components come together, when 'the unity of method penetrates the work as a whole', the result is not just a 'unity of opposites' but a 'new, higher unity'.[73] *Ivan the Terrible* was Eisenstein's laboratory for exploring these techniques. His theoretical work of the 1940s, written during and after shooting *Ivan the Terrible*, and his specific analysis of structures in *Ivan*, form the first extended analysis among film theorists of the way in which films function as a whole. This body of writing, which guides the analysis below, was the first attempt to explain how every element in a film, every formal and narrative technique, combines to create an overall effect.[74]

The setting

Ivan the Terrible takes place in a setting defined by architecture, wall paintings and bas-reliefs, royal and everyday objects, clothing, jewelry and furniture. Most of the action occurs indoors and the rare outdoor scenes are constructed more like stage sets than natural spaces. It is immediately apparent that this is an artificial world in which people do not act naturally. The strangeness of individual characters seems to be connected with the artificiality and strangeness of the setting in which they operate.

The palace architecture makes most indoor space seem closed and claustrophobia-inducing. The few exceptions (the Polish court, the cathedral during the Coronation) emphasize by contrast the claustrophobia induced by Ivan's palaces in Moscow and Alexandrova Sloboda. This is a central practice in *Ivan*: we appreciate the essence of something by experiencing its absence. The palace architecture, with its arched entryways and stairways, its small chambers leading off to smaller chambers, its surprisingly elongated or truncated rooms, was inspired by a set of drawings by the Italian draughtsman and architect, Giovanni Piranesi, which Eisenstein analyzed in some detail.[75] Eisenstein noted the way Piranesi captured the essence of certain architectural forms (arches, stairways and the spaces they contained) and then 'exploded' those forms in drawings that seem to reach into another dimension. The almost infinite repetition of structural enclosures, like an image reflected in doubled mirrors, has the paradoxical effect of implying both the confinement of constructions and the infinity of space. In *Ivan* people continually escape down corridors, along shafts of light, and through the palace's tiny mousehole-doorways. But they must squeeze themselves through diminishing spaces to do so. Emergence (and the rebirth symbolized in these emergences), is difficult and traumatic but possible. In Eisenstein's analysis of Piranesi's drawings, the explosion of form allows us to see both the form itself and, by 'making it strange', all the qualities contained in the form. Stone is both stone and something more than stone. The distorted spaces in Ivan's palaces invite us behind the surface narrative to characterize the claustrophobia and paranoia that go unmentioned in the dialogue, and to reinforce the dangers of conspiracies and secrets. The physical environment not only shapes the characters' actions, but it expresses characters' fears and possibilities. This effect is profoundly magnified by the decorations on the walls.

The wall decorations in *Ivan the Terrible* are among the film's most striking features. Frescos, tapestries, bas-reliefs and painted icons surround the action with Russian Orthodox images. Some of the images are derived directly from Orthodox icons. Many of the props were authentic sixteenth-century objects lent to Eisenstein for the production. Others are variations of well-known biblical themes designed for the film. All of the images are exaggerated or stylized.

The icons function like much of the other visual material, as references to the film's themes (resurrection, maternal love, judgment, salvation, damnation) and as clues to character and action. As with the architecture, Eisenstein wanted the religious imagery to have the effect of pointing to surfaces and suggesting depths. 'All the frescos (in the film) – without inordinate *insisting* – should *thematically* ... correspond to what is happening in the scene. As if *composed (in the musical sense of the word)* of that which is happening around them.'[76] Accordingly, Ivan's confession occurs before a huge fresco of the Last Judgment; scenes involving surveillance take place under watchful eyes; Efrosinia and Pimen are paired with dark angels and devils; Anastasia is associated with the Mother of God; Vladimir Staritsky is set up to be murdered beneath a ceiling depicting the Forty Martyrs. The religious imagery also serves to link characters with each other and with specific actions. Anastasia dies under a tapestry of the Holy Mother and Child and her murder is discussed twice by Fedor (Anastasia's substitute) under two different icons of the Holy Mother and Child, all of which recall Ivan's mother's embrace before she died and foreshadow Efrosinia's embrace of Vladimir after he dies.

The associations are not always so explicit. Resurrection images are common: Lazarus (in the cathedral at the Coronation), Jonah (in the chapel at the end of Part II), and the Last Judgment (in the cathedral behind Vladimir's murder and before Ivan's confession). They suggest various forms of rebirth: Russia's rebirth as a great power on the Baltic, Ivan's rebirth as tsar and as Satan, Vladimir's rebirth as a martyr (albeit a guilty one). These altered and loosely linked repetitions create an ambiguity that serves Eisenstein's purposes of arousing the viewer's curiosity, forcing us to looker harder and think again, and engaging us emotionally. Eisenstein used these methods literally in depicting Ivan's childhood fears. 'In the Prologue,' he wrote, the frescos 'should be especially excessively large in scale; in this they should reflect the *sensations* they produced in the *young* Ivan. In *his* imagination they are extra-grandiose, colossal, threatening. And their residual effect should be identical: in the scene of the Last Judgment, where again Ivan experiences his childhood fears.'[77]

The most unusual and instructive icon in *Ivan the Terrible* is the angel that covers the entire ceiling of Ivan's throne room in the Golden Palace. Seen in the Prologue and again in the meeting between Ivan and Filipp, the angel is a composite figure, linked with Archangel Michael and the Angel of Apocalypse,[78] which Eisenstein used to deploy a suggestive field of images and religious motifs as seeds of Ivan's story. A simple description of the angel or a brief glimpse of it shows that it contains much of what is to come. The figure is elongated, fragmented and impossible to perceive whole in a single shot. Its face is a sun with a fiery corona for a halo while its feet dangle before a serene, sleepy moon at the other end of the hall. The explosive power in the fiery head contrasts with the tender vulnerability of the out-turned feet and placid moon, a contrast reinforced by a lingering shot of young Ivan's feet, vainly stretching out to reach the floor and retracting. And if our perception works the way Eienstein wanted it to work, those feet will recall the feet of the saint dangling above Ivan in the first scene of the Prologue. Neither entirely male or female, entirely religious or secular, the angel is both warrior (the sword) and judge (scales). So this image is elusive, androgynous, dualistic, dynamic and intriguing. But this hardly accounts for the power of the unusual fresco or Eisenstein's great satisfaction with it. The angel's mysterious power (and the source of Eisenstein's pleasure) lies in the complexity just beneath its visible surface and an unusual combination of motifs drawn from a variety of sources.

This is no ordinary Archangel Michael, but specifically the Michael of the Apocalypse; and it is no ordinary Apocalypse, but the Apocalypse (and the angels) represented at the historical Ivan's palaces at Alexandrova Sloboda and the Kremlin. Unlike *Ivan*'s ceiling angel, the most common images of Michael portray him in profile, either facing Jesus on an iconostasis or in flight, as in the well-known fresco above the doorway to the Uspensky Cathedral in the Kremlin. Most icons of the Apocalypse (especially the more durable ones painted on wood and reproduced in books) are orderly, ritualized affairs. But Eisenstein knew from reading and possibly from visiting Alexandrova Sloboda (which had been open as a museum since 1921), that Ivan the Terrible had

21. Angel of the Apocalypse.

surrounded himself with images of the Apocalypse both at the Kremlin in Moscow and at Alexandrova. And if Eisenstein visited the site (which I think he must have done) he would have found a messier, less symmetrical fresco of the Apocalypse (with some very exotic monsters) in the Pokrovsky Cathedral there. He would also have seen a beautiful, unusual fresco of a frontal Michael and the other archangels painted against a rare black background, and an eighteenth-century painting of the Apocalypse, in which Michael, in accordance with a specific text from Revelation, is standing on a sun, the flames of which are like those on the angel in the film. He would also have found a rare Michael with scales, a hell-mouth just like the one on his Last Judgment, as well as a prototype for a small detail found on one of the icons he designed for his Uspensky Cathedral of the devil Michael hurled in to the flames. The Apocalyptic iconography at Alexandrova Sloboda, with its suns and moons, its monsters and angels, its monstrous and heavenly rebirths, and especially its ultimate judgment, are all planted here in the opening scenes of *Ivan the Terrible*. Not only does the angel foreshadow all the themes and structures of the film, it sets up the ultimate criteria for judging Ivan's life.

But when you look back at the angel there are still a few loose ends. Except for the wings, and perhaps the scales, it hardly resembles a religious figure at all. Scales are associated with Michael, but more commonly in Western Christian than Russian Orthodox iconography. And the angel is a thing of nature: sun, moon, clouds and stars. So it is curious to learn that just days before drawing his definitive sketch for the angel, Eisenstein read and bookmarked a chapter in Igor Grabar's *History of Russian Art* describing a series of controversial frescos painted in Ivan's time on those same walls and ceiling of the Golden Palace. Highly unusual for their secular subjects, these frescos formed a 'complex allegorical cycle', according to Grabar.[79] The entrance halls were covered with scenes of battle and statecraft, specifically intended to teach a young tsar to behave. Like Eisenstein's angel, the ideal ruler is depicted as a youthful hero, both fearsome warrior and virtuous judge (sword and scales again). The Golden Palace itself was decorated with an assembly of allegorical figures, all of which represented either natural cycles or dualisms. On the ceiling, surrounding a portrait of Christ, were the figures of Reason (*razum*) as a young woman writing on a scroll and Insanity (*bezumie*), a naked man with clothes askew. Lust is there and Justice too: a girl holding scales, of course. Further along are figures representing Earth, Wind and Fire, and Spring, Summer, Fall and Winter, none of whom is fully dressed, all of which culminate finally in Death. As Eisenstein read these pages, he must have appreciated the irony in Grabar's argument that the didactic and secular style of painting represented here, along with a famous unsuccessful attempt by one cleric to have the shockingly fleshy paintings removed, marked a shift towards increasing state control of icon painting.[80] But more important, these earthy, secular images explain the natural element of Eisenstein's angel and offer another, slightly different but related source of the themes it represents: the circularity of power, the duality of character and the ultimate necessity of facing judgment.

The secular images do not simply reiterate what the religious sources had conveyed. Repetition deepens and complicates the context in which Ivan operates: all of Ivan and all the possibilities he will face are contained in the deeper recessive suggestions layered into this angel. This most artificial construction suggests the infinitely variable possibilities of real life. Narrative and structure are again inseparable. Just as the angel contains all of Ivan's possibilities, ready for him to choose which of its cyclical or dualistic paths he will follow, it also plants in the depths of our perception all the possible stories and meanings that we will dredge up when we need to make sense of what comes later on. Eisenstein packed all these layers into his design but he did not necessarily assume that as viewers we would have access to all of them at once. He did expect viewers to apprehend complex images in all their complexity at some level. Even objects that cannot be identified and explained can tug on the psyche and contribute to one's overall response to the film

Objects of other kinds also function like the frescos. They take on meaning outside the usual pragmatic and even symbolic functions and their images plant little bombs to explode later. The camera lingers on them, lighting fetishizes them, and things in general acquire the status of character: goblets, chairs, coats, hats, crosses, rings and earrings, among many others, play a role in the apprehensive experience and development of the narrative.

The double-headed eagle, adopted by Ivan III, Ivan's grandfather, as the dynastic emblem, is associated in the film primarily with Ivan; it both signifies Russian power and becomes an external sign of Ivan's inner dualism. Necks link Maliuta, Vladimir, Ivan and the Kolychev martyrs but signify different things for each of them: Ivan's threatened wrath on the one hand and the tsar's own fears and remorse on the other. The necks also provide a link to the arms and legs that stretch tentatively from sleeves and hems of caftans, all of which suggest a yearning for transition or a cautious hint of a transformation to come. Ivan's hands stretch out of their sleeves across a white furry coverlet when he realizes that he killed his wife with his own hands. They appear as almost abstract objects, reaching out beyond this world trying to touch Anastasia in the next.

Some objects are associated with the opposite of their usual meaning. Rings and earrings signify vast wealth and all the boyars wear them, but Eisenstein also used them to blur gender roles. In one note about a scene that did not materialize, he has Alexei Basmanov discover Fedor wearing an earring. While muttering a few phrases about the holiness of the *oprichniki*, he socks Fedor in the ear.[81] Crosses are often associated with unholy behavior: Kurbsky kisses a cross at a moment of supreme hypocrisy and Eisenstein knew that the *oprichniki* often dressed in monastic garb in order to mock the faithful. Peter Volynets and young Ivan wear the same small wooden cross and they clasp it similarly after their experience of 'first blood'.

Of all the objects that resonate across levels and types of meaning and insist that we watch the film with heightened attention, none supersedes the eyes. Eyes are full-fledged characters in *Ivan*. They appear as objects, gestures, symbols and metaphors in almost every scene.

First and foremost the eye is a universal symbol of the camera. The film camera is our eye, the tool we use to participate in making the film's meaning. In one of Eisenstein's first important theoretical publications, he argued against a passive function for the motion picture camera, against the idea that the camera might record 'life unawares', a stance associated with Dziga Vertov's 'Cine-eye'. Eisenstein wrote in rebuttal, 'We don't need a Cine-eye, we need a Cine-fist.'[82] The aggressive eyes of *Ivan the Terrible* are Eisenstein's transformation of that eye into a fist. *Ivan*'s eyes are anything but passive instruments; the camera looks back at us as we watch what it has captured. Eyes gaze on us from the walls and ceilings, they keep track of illicit goings on, they trace potential transformations, control friends and enemies alike, and they stare in terror at death. This cine-eye extends our gaze into the action, the same way Maliuta extends the tsar's eye. The eye of God, the eye of the tsar, the eye of the tsar's henchman, the inner eye all keep reminding us that we are watching and judging what others are doing. There is no neutral stance, no exterior point of view; we cannot escape judgment any more than Ivan can.

Perhaps the eye's most striking and ubiquitous role is solo: the single eye, its twin covered by hands, hair, props, clothing and shadows. Eisenstein gives us no direct guidance in interpreting this gesture but the single eye must be the ultimate metaphor for ironic ambivalence: is this gaze half-full or half-empty? Is one eye open or one eye closed? In terms of narrative, the political, the psychological and the philosophical meet here, in the ambivalence of the single eye.

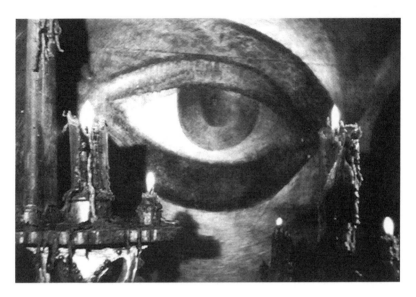

22. Surveillance.

The single eye is almost always associated with treachery. The slimy Livonian Ambassador is the first character to cover an eye, with one of his dark eyeglass frames down. Next Efrosinia plots in the arched door-way, one eye darkened by shadow. Then Anastasia lowers her face into her sleeve after flirting with Kurbsky. Ivan, on his deathbed, peers out from under the Bible at the treachery around him with a watchful, scared eye. He lies back down and covers both eyes, also a bad sign: he covers both eyes just after Vladimir's murder.

Seeing with only one eye would suggest political blindness even if Russians did not have the proverb: 'Ignore the past and you lose an eye, forget the past and you lose both eyes.' The past bears on the present but only if one looks (and even then it is not clear how the present proceeded from the past). Some characters are scared to look, some are oblivious to their blinkers, others choose not to look too hard. Kurbsky hides his disloyalty behind one eye, Maliuta is blind to Ivan's flaws, and Peter cannot bear to see the bizarre reversal about to save him after plotting and indeed killing the tsar. And who could walk around Moscow in Eisenstein's lifetime with both eyes open and survive? But what sort of survival is this? In the film, self-protection is a retreat from responsibility, a sign of shame and treachery.

For Eisenstein, seeing with only one eye is limiting because it precludes irony. Only Ivan 'sees everything from two angles; essential, by the way, in the *ironic* attitude'.[83] Ironically, half-sight also seems to negate the apparently infinite expansion of meanings conveyed by the repetition and mirroring of the majority of other objects in the film. Everything else, from beards to toes, functions within an expanding universe of meanings, but most of the time, the film's characters can only half-see the world around them.

Conversely, and perhaps more important, the restriction of sight can also increase the possibilities for a fluidity and multiplicity of meanings. Seeing too much imprisons the objects of our sight in the totality of our gaze, just as surveillance imprisons the objects of a totalitarian state. Seeing just a little or only a fragment endows the object of sight with some power to escape labeling, to resist petrification, to change into something else. Seeing in fragments allows multiple unforeseen associations to emerge. Being seen only partially allows us a measure of freedom, an escape from surveillance.[84]

Eyes in *Ivan* can see too much. With eyes wide open, Ivan glares in anger or threat. Before significant episodes of resurrection, Ivan and Vladimir both lean back, lift their heads and stare down at their fate in terror. Seeing eye to eye allows characters to communicate, as Ivan, Fedor and Maliuta convey the assassin's presence at the feast. Failure to meet another's eyes just as clearly signals misunderstanding: Ivan and Filipp do not meet each other's gaze when Ivan begs Filipp for his friendship. Then they burn each other with looks of penetrating hatred before the fiery furnace.

Eyes in *Ivan* seem to have a life of their own. They move almost independently of their owners. Up and down, from side to side, slowly and swiftly, eyes draw lines inside their sockets, around the spaces their bodies inhabit, and to the depths beyond. In two rhyming close-ups, at the end of the Coronation and the end of the fiery furnace scene, Ivan's eyes chart a semicircular path along the top arch of his eyes. These particular eye movements mark highly significant moments in Ivan's serial rebirths, in his self-definition as tsar. Eisenstein associated such outlines, or 'contour' lines with a fundamental demarcation of identity. In his study of Disney's animation, Eisenstein saw the ability of contour lines to flow and shift as signs of our ability to change form, to escape rigidly defined identities and embrace change.[85]

Eisenstein's ideas about our dynamic ability to change form are also contained in the film's costumes. Like architecture and icons, costumes are more than mere body coverings denoting period fashion or individual taste. Boyars and *oprichniki* dress in clearly contrasting styles denoting

23. Maliuta, dressed in boyar brocade.

class difference, but the *oprichniki* gradually adopt features of boyar dress, as they establish their 'neo-feudal' order and move into positions of power. Their tunics become more decorative and more luxurious until they resemble costumes associated with boyars. Maliuta first appears in the ragged dress of a rebellious commoner. After the battle at Kazan, he changes into a uniform — the high-shouldered, eagle-like uniform of the tsar's aide – to skulk around the palace as the tsar's eye during Ivan's deathbed scenes. In Part II, the simple black tunic of the *oprichniki* has become a fancier, pleated affair, and the young men wear fur-trimmed hats and cloaks. Maliuta wears a bulky fur coat over a tunic of boyar brocade at the execution of the Kolychevs, and by the end of Part II at the feast, Maliuta wears a coat of boyar brocade as well, as does Alexei Basmanov. The *oprichniki* themselves trade in their black tunics for red and gold at the feast and then cover those with black monks' robes during the procession at the end of Part II. Ivan changes into a monk's garb when it suits him to appear repentant, at the fiery furnace and after having Vladimir murdered, but it always seems a mockery, a 'costume'.

Eisenstein also calls attention to the putting on and taking off of clothes. Sometimes this indicates the covering of vulnerability with a disguise of official authority, as with the young Ivan during the Prologue. More often the act of dressing reveals or covers up an authentic (private) self under an official (public) mask. Efrosinia significantly discards her black robe to reveal a white gown when she adopts her maternal role and sings to her son. Maliuta, using the same gesture, discards his fur coat to reveal his blended *oprichnik*-boyar executioner's uniform just before beheading the first Kolychev. Ivan's fur coat often connotes his official public self and he sheds it when he wants to let himself feel some authentic emotion. As a sign of ambivalence about the conflict between his public and private selves, sitting alone with his astrolabe Ivan starts to put on a fur-trimmed cloak and wears it slung over his shoulder when he gets up. (The fur–power link is reiterated in the lyrics to Efrosinia's lullaby.) At the end of Part I, Maliuta and Fedor dress Ivan before he goes out to meet the people and display himself in various artificially staged poses: a ritual display of power that disguises the fact that he has created a secret army to support him in the *oprichniki*. And when Vladimir Staritsky dresses in the tsar's clothes, the garb transforms him: suddenly he wants power.

Costumes together with objects, then, suggest endless possibilities for character change in *Ivan the Terrible*. Class, gender, morality and loyalty are all costumes that can be exchanged at will, offering us a field of choices. But Eisenstein distinguishes between mere exchange and a kind of transformation that is more profound, and for his aesthetics, more significant. Class and gender, for example, are depicted as binary pairs; a change of disguise can affect a switch to the other pole of identity. But such simple binary exchanges in the film lead to disaster: the *oprichnik* leaders' costume change is a sign of their neo-feudalism; Vladimir's disguise as tsar leads to his death; Efrosinia discards her black robe to reveal the white underneath but her maternal role is deadly for Vladimir and destroys her as well. Fedor's disguise as Anastasia calls attention to the artificiality of the change; his womanly form is rigid and false, especially in contrast to his face, beneath the doll-like mask, which is highly mobile and expressive as are the androgynous men around him, dancing with marked suppleness and dynamism. Binary costume changes, ironically, convey choice as a non-choice, a mere reversal of fixed rigid identities. On the other hand, the androgynous ambiguity of the tunic/ dresses of the dancing *oprichniki*, the sinister seductiveness of their leader, the smiles masking the threat of their song all collapse binary oppositions. By merging gendered attributes, rather than simply exchanging them, they offer much more complex and fluid possibilities for identity.[86]

Shadows further develop Eisenstein's notions of unfixed identity and the possibilities for escape from the forms we are given. The shadow is a natural metaphor for our ability to change shape. In almost every scene, shadows witness the action and offer a slightly altered version of events occurring before them. The shadows are almost always larger than the people who cast them: they watch and judge. They seem to be both more powerful and, in important ways, freer than the people who cast them. As they fly off in their own directions, they allow us to imagine different versions of the narratives they reflect. In the most spectacular cases, the shadows take on a life of their own. When Ivan strides down the hall to discuss foreign policy with his ambassador, Nepeya, in Part I, he is not only dwarfed by his shadow, the shadow seems actually to free itself from Ivan's body. Since this scene is Ivan's first appearance after his key resurrection from death, his shadows take on another meaning. If the Christ-like figure who died is resurrected as Satan, his enormous and independent shadow suggests a path that might have been taken had Ivan not sold his soul to the Devil in order to preserve the Great Russian State. The shadow world is a visual sign that Ivan's path was not predetermined, that he and the other characters made choices in a realm of possibilities. They are an ever-present reminder that even within worlds of surveillance and constricted movements, of tiny mousehole doorways that force us to bend to an arbitrary will, we make choices and those choices have consequences.[87]

Eisenstein also believed that shape-shifting shadows, like the animated figures of Walt Disney's early films, conveyed an escape from conventional identity. The freedom rooted in the fluidity of the form itself, he thought, represented the 'freedom from all categories, all conventions'. The ability of animated characters and shadows to change shape, to twist, stretch and shrink, made a mockery of fixed form, 'a rejection of once-and-forever allotted form, freedom from ossification, the ability to dynamically assume any form'.[88] It is no wonder that Eisenstein peopled Ivan with shadows: if shadows potentially contain all forms, including images and their opposites, they are the ideal metaphor for the sense of identity Eisenstein wanted to convey. He saw (or wanted to see) human identity as an irreducible contradiction, but not a dead-end. We shift like cartoons or shadows among our various identities: male/female, public/private, good/evil. Only at moments when we achieve a perfect correspondence between our oppositions, can they collapse into each other and offer us *ekstasis*.

Acting

Ivan the Terrible is in large part a study of Ivan's inner divisions and his personal impact on his country, but Eisenstein's actors do not convey inner states in any conventional actorly manner. Instead, the actors' physical gestures and body movements are treated as 'objects' analogous to the artifacts that surround them. I have already described how eye gestures function in the same way as objects: linking characters, conveying ideas, representing personal attributes and relationships, and hinting at the director's theoretical positions. Eisenstein treats his actors as formal elements of shot composition. Many viewers find this acting style overly intellectual and unappealing. But the accumulation of such effects, the merging of people with the physical setting, can be oddly affecting. Though some viewers might find the overly stylized acting as unanimated and bloodless, one might alternatively notice the animation of the material surroundings as reaching a state of equilibrium with the human actors. The de-humanization of the people and the humanization of the objects create a 'unity of opposites' that is surprisingly moving. The actors' unnatural movements, which turn people into objects with the same status as their clothing or furniture, actually heighten our awareness of their essential humanness, an irony that fascinated Eisenstein. Their form achieves an independence from their identity that, in turn, distills and reflects the essence of their identity.[89]

Specific gestures form a whole network of independent, interrelated signs. Some gestures are shorthand for action. Several characters employ the 'double-look'. During the rebellion, Ivan looks at the crowd, first to observe and then, opening his eyes wider, gives a second look, to command (the people kneel). Some gestures are intended to link characters in similar situations with similar significance: characters facing death in *Ivan* face death with the same expression and posture: arched back, face tilted up, eyes wide open staring down. Some gestures have specific metaphorical meanings: characters rise when they are rising in power and sink when they are defeated. All the actors move unnaturally but in such similarly patterned ways. They alternate between slow-motion (or no motion, shown only in different postures and positions in sequential shots) and rapid-fire, frenzied motion, whipping around or sliding their eyes or throwing up their hands. Their body motions are segmented: limb movements are at odds with torsos, heads move separately from bodies.

All these movements allude more generally to the deeper structures of the film: repetition, emotional intensification, the accumulation of significance and the contradictory essence in absence. Contorted motions and exaggerated gestures extend the impact of the shadows' fluidity. The strange movements, such as bending, stretching, twisting and arching, show bodies coerced and constricted. But at the same time, such unnatural movement emphasizes the body's extremes, and extreme abilities

24. Ivan chooses death.

to defy natural form. Actors stretch out for freedom, lurch back from danger and hurtle to collide in intimacy or threat. Abrupt transitions call attention to the very possibility of transition, while compelling us to remember that change is wrenching.

Editing, camerawork, and shot composition
The formal techniques used to construct *Ivan the Terrible* show us the evolution of Eisenstein's cinematic practice most clearly. Editing discontinuities, unusual camera placement and frame composition are all critical elements in constructing, deepening and enhancing our perception of the lines already discussed. Eisenstein was fascinated by the ways he had developed and complicated these strategies since his earliest montage experiments.

In *The Battleship Potemkin*, for example, an intense experience of grief for the fallen sailor, Vakulinchuk, was produced by the dynamic juxtaposition of images of different individuals grieving. In *Ivan the Terrible*, the tsar's grief is conveyed and intensified first by diverse shots of just the one figure. We do not see Ivan moving around Anastasia's coffin. We see relatively static images of him in distinct postures of grief. This scene's power is derived, Eisenstein believed, from the splitting of Ivan's grief into separate components and reuniting them in a montage series of shots. The series is a carefully planned sequence that matches the emotional and narrative purpose of the scene. The camera cranes down on Ivan in the opening shot, depicting him in successively lower shots until the moment of ultimate despair and ecstatic transformation ('Is this not divine punishment') through the demonic resurrection ('You lie!') to the tsar's rise to renewed power, standing up on the coffin platform, arms stretched upward ('for the Great Russian State').[90]

But montage in *Ivan* develops the earlier silent montage by adding a network of associations produced by other visual elements within the frame: the rhythm of camerawork and editing, the dialog and music (and later, color). Eisenstein believed that he succeeded in producing *pathos* and *ekstasis* in *Ivan the Terrible* because every single element in this complex polyphonic construction was governed by the same compositional principle and immersed in the same emotional principle.[91] In this scene that principle is despair, and the conquering of despair (for the film as a whole, it was *power*). In the coffin scene, the polyphonic readings by Pimen and Maliuta intensify Ivan's despair until he reaches the point of ecstatic transition and leaps to a 'higher unity'.

Eisenstein uses two kinds of editing, disorientation and repetition, to coordinate the visual with the thematic and the psychological. In the coffin scene, most of the disorienting cues occur while Ivan is in despair, most of the doubling and repetition occur after he has conquered despair and is rising to his demonic, superhuman stature. The scene at the coffin opens with spatial disorientation. The coffin itself is on a platform that is impossibly, absurdly tall and it is surrounded by strangely tall black candles (which will reappear in every death scene and every *oprichnik* scene from here on, linking the *oprichniki* with death and with a reversal of holy and ubiquitous use of candles characteristic of Russian Orthodoxy). A crane-shot from above the coffin descends to locate Ivan slumped and powerless at its feet. Ivan seems small until he conquers his despair. Unlike in the Coronation and almost every other scene, Ivan is a shrinking, unstable center at first. Pimen, on the other hand, looms powerfully in the foreground, reading his disheartening psalm, and Maliuta appears in close-up, both shot from below, emphasizing their power over Ivan. Ivan is even shown out of focus behind Pimen. Efrosinia lurks in the shadows, Maliuta and the Basmanovs emerge from the shadows behind Ivan. Every shot is taken from a different angle and each angle is an extreme. Ironically, the very distinctness of each shot is what makes their ultimate merging that much more powerful.

Eisenstein emphasizes these disparities with space/time discontinuities. The first shot, for example, places Ivan on Anastasia's right. Pimen's continuous reading makes us think that no time has passed between shots but we next see Ivan on the other side of the coffin. This happens again during his resurrection from despair. Ivan tilts his head back in the Christ-like death posture (echoing precisely his posture on his deathbed), he drops his head in anger and turns to face the coffin, standing at about the middle of the coffin. Pimen reads throughout that shot and into the next, but when we see Ivan again he is turning back towards us (still angry, about to explode with 'You lie!'), from a position at the head of the coffin, where he knocks over the candlesticks. One effect of this move (the disjuncture of his response) is to mute the anger that brings him back to life and confuse us about its cause. Was it Kurbsky's betrayal? The specific lines of the psalm? Suspicions about Anastasia? Or that the boyars were rousing the people against him?

Disorienting shots disappear briefly, while Ivan is hatching the plan to establish the *oprichnina*, replaced by techniques that emphasize Ivan's power. The Basmanovs gaze at Ivan with the same gaze of blind trust Anastasia used. The camera is fairly stable, but it now uses techniques that amplify rather than diminish Ivan's power. Twice the editing cuts an action in mid-motion and repeats a tiny fraction of it, from a slightly altered angle. At the moment when Ivan takes Basmanov's suggestion and transforms it into his own plan, he contradicts Alexei and Maliuta, twice telling them that he will not return to Moscow as a soldier but will rely on the people. Just as Ivan repeats the line ('not as a soldier'), he is shown rising up above his two henchmen. He bends up into the frame, the shot is cut when he is partway up, the camera inches in, and he is shown in a new shot repeating a fraction of his rise and unbending all the way up. A similar but even more powerful example occurs at the end of the scene when Ivan's power is reestablished in almost mythic proportions. He receives Fedor's 'You are right!' and climbs up behind the coffin to fling his arms in the air in the tsar's power gesture. The camera cuts to his rising again, even more dynamically, and again, with yet more energy. Then turning to face the *oprichniki* flooding into the cathedral, who seem to have emerged fully formed from his imagination, another disorienting cut occurs. That previous series of shots took place at the foot of the coffin; now Ivan is shot from behind and appears in long-shot standing on the side of the coffin, watching the arrival of his new army. The effect is both to diminish him, and amaze us with the power of his dedication, to both affirm and challenge our perception of all that greatness and power. Doubt is reinforced thematically by shots of Alexei and Fedor gazing blindly at Ivan and by his final kiss to Anastasia. Though it is implied that she supports the Great Cause still, this appears to be a kiss goodbye as Ivan trades his angel Anastasia for his demon Fedor and the frightening men of the *oprichniki*.

The emotional and compositional elements come together here in the variations on the theme of the 'unity of opposites', in this case power and weakness. Examples of such disorienting and reinforcing camerawork appear throughout the film. At the Coronation, Kurbsky and Kolychev switch positions in between shots. At the execution of the Kolychevs, the music suggests temporal continuity, but Maliuta has had time to finish his work and put away his sword and Ivan and Fedor have had time to dress in fur coats and hats before entering the courtyard. Doubling or slightly altered repetition of movements also recurs frequently: for example, when Ivan is leaving his palace at Alexandrova Sloboda to go out and greet the people, Maliuta and Fedor dress him in his fur coat, and as he moves forward, the camera cuts to a slightly different position and he again moves forward, out of the frame.

In the feast scene, two different time schemes face each other in counterpoint: Fedor's dynamic direction of the dancers and Ivan's patient, interrupted, maneuvering of Vladimir. The dance seems to proceed in real time without interruptions, continuing while we are watching Ivan and the party at the table. But Ivan's conversations at the other end of the hall seem to stretch out over a much longer period of time as Vladimir drinks, talks and falls asleep.

Occasionally, disorienting and doubling shots work together. At the Coronation, when Ivan announces that the Church will be under his control, we see Pimen's reaction in two shots. First in medium long-shot, from slightly below we see Pimen move forward and to our left, towards us and towards the center of the church as if in disbelief and to hear better. The camera cuts back to Ivan speaking, then back to Pimen, but now the camera is closer, lower and the frame is at first empty. Pimen moves quickly into the frame and in the opposite direction, off to our right, and away from us, into a much darker space. It is as if Ivan's words had lured him out and then knocked him back. The tight focus of the second shot is disorienting and the rapid movement is intense. We feel Pimen's shock as he blurs out of focus past us and then he is further diminished when Ivan shifts to a new subject while we are still looking at Pimen.

Another kind of repetition Eisenstein used extensively in Ivan is the 'axial' cut as in the shot sequence of the spying Maliuta holding his eye open.[92] (See illustration 5, 'The Eye of the State'.) The camera moves 'on an axis' straight towards him, but in separate cuts, each image larger than the last as the camera approaches. This sort of axial sequence goes beyond calling our attention; it forces us to take in its artificiality and it intensifies, in a mechanical, noticeable way, the emotional power of the image and narrative power of the idea the image refers to. It also reinforces our sense of swooping in on the action or swooping out towards the viewer. Characters rush towards or pull away from us. Efrosinia seems especially prone to throw herself towards us or be approached in extreme close-up by the camera. She flies into the meeting hatching the conspiracy against Ivan, going out of focus as she approaches. The camera takes us right into her face when Maliuta enters her chambers bringing the empty goblet and an invitation to the feast.

Another form of disorientation occurs between sequences. Eisenstein wanted episodes 'to collide' with one another precisely the way individual shots had collided in *Potemkin*.[93] Some episodes follow each other without clear explanation. One minute Ivan is celebrating victory over Kazan, the next he is dying. Where did that sweet baby come from and what became of him? Even when episodes do follow logically, they collide in tempo, style or spatial cues.

Eisenstein used this array of disruptive and reinforcing techniques systematically in *Ivan* and they form the basis for a technical unity. Disorientation and repetition in technique form a system of disruptions that match the interruptions in the narrative and psychological realms, immersing the narrative in a unified system of formal techniques. Composition within the shot is also permeated with formal representations of the 'unity of opposites'.

Double or mirror images appear probably more than any other motif in *Ivan*. Double close-up shots, from every conceivable angle, link characters together thematically or sexually, and link pairs of characters together to suggest moral correspondences. Ivan appears face to face and cheek to cheek with every single character in the film and many of these images are mirrored in his face to face encounters with other characters. Ivan's face to face with Fedor can mirror images of father and son, husband and wife, old friend or bitter enemy. Efrosinia's caress of her son's head in her lap during her lullaby is repeated in Ivan's caress of Vladimir at the banquet table.

Triangles also abound, evoking the dialectical nature of *ekstasis*: opposites collapse to produce a higher unity. These triangles are sometimes suggested, as with Ivan standing between Anastasia in her coffin and Fedor kneeling on the ground, but they are represented as well, as in the coffin scene, with its fertile ground for dialectical resurrections, where they abound: Pimen/Maliuta/Ivan; Alexei/Maliuta/Ivan; Alexei/Ivan/Fedor; Ivan/Anastasia/their children, the *oprichniki*. These occur through-

25. Ivan paired.

out the film from Kurbsky and Kolychev pouring coins over Ivan, to Shuisky and Belsky arguing over the head of young Ivan, to Fedor and Ivan winking over the head of Vladimir sitting on the throne, dressed to kill. However, none of these triangles produced desirable 'children' or higher unities. The struggles for Ivan's soul that were represented in this triangular form resulted in monstrous or demonic births.

Eisenstein, a master of black/white contrast, was fascinated by the possibilities of color, which he used in the same deliberate way he used other elements of shot composition as repeatable, interpenetrable markers of meaning. Never content with simple backgrounds, he used black-and-white to convey moral positions and other dualisms and he used color to denote mood, theme, character and sensation.

'Black is connected with darkness, night, cold, and, like it or not, it evokes negative feelings,' he argued in a lecture on the subject.[94] Although he occasionally uses black ironically in *Ivan*, for the most part black is associated with evil and white with goodness. Efrosinia's costuming provides a good example. In Part I, her clothes are increasingly dominated by black. She wears white at the Coronation and the wedding; then she shifts to black with a decreasing amount of gold and brocade decoration. At Ivan's deathbed, she wears black with great deal of gold embroidery. Back in her palace, on her own 'throne', as boyars complain about Ivan's actions after his resurrection, she is almost entirely in black, with just a little gold trim on her headdress. She wears a totally black cloak over her brocade gown at Anastasia's bedside while poisoning her and the same black cloak hiding in the corner during the coffin scene before darting away into the flames. In Part II, she almost always wears multi-colored clothing. All this leads up to two crucial moments. When Pimen informs her that he is going to let Filipp die because he is more useful as a dead martyr than a living ally, even Efrosinia is horrified by his inhuman cynicism. 'White is the cowl, black is the soul,' she mutters. Pimen had been the only one in this scene wearing any white, and he was wearing a black cloak under his white hood, which was unusual for him. Even more interesting, Efrosinia turns from Pimen's exit towards Vladimir and as she does so she conspicuously discards her black headdress and cloak, revealing her tiny core of goodness, her underlying maternal heart.

Eisenstein was opposed to using color merely to enhance verisimilitude. He used the Agfacolor film stock captured from the Germans at the end of the war as yet another element of linkage to identify and intensify each of the themes and emotions depicted in the 'Feast of the *Oprichniki*'. One can imagine the whirling men, frenzied music and coy mixture of flirtation and threat in Fedor's song in black-and-white, and it would remain a powerful sequence, but the addition of color heightens our sense of its contradictory qualities. The red glow that envelops all the action in the scene turns the banquet hall into a chamber of hell. Red is picked up by Ivan's red and gold patterned caftan, and by the red background saturating the icons of the Forty Martyrs on the ceiling. The vivid contrast of gold, red and black *oprichnik* tunics adds to the patterned and chaotic qualities of the dance and to the contrast with Fedor's white caftan and mask. Basmanov's face is flooded with red when he asks Ivan if they are not bound by ties of blood shed. And Vladimir's face, in the characteristic 'death look', with head flung back, eyes down, is dramatically flooded blue, after looking through the portal to his own death.

The transition back to black-and-white is also handled with a color transition. This minute scene is another good example of Eisenstein's use of disorientation and doubling. The gold-tunicked *oprichniki* bow down to Vladimir twice, but each time they face in a different direction, for no apparent reason. This both recalls the original Coronation when the people bow to Ivan in the crowded cathedral and contrasts with it, since a red glow replaces rays of sunlight, and of course they bow to a false tsar. Temporal distortion is conveyed by the continuity of music and of Ivan's speech but Vladimir is sound asleep and then, before time can pass, *oprichniki* already dressed in black monks' cowls are filing through the bowing, gold *oprichniki*. The reduction to two tones, black and gold, begins the transition back to black-and-white.

All the formal techniques I have discussed can be roughly divided into two categories: those that link and those that disrupt linkages. Incessant repetition and reiteration is met with equally incessant dislocation and disorientation. This underlying structural method, yet another 'unity of opposites', provides the foundation for the political and psychological forms of unity discussed in previous chapters.[95] And, as in the political and the psychological, each of these opposites contains elements of the other: the excess of repetition is disorienting, and examples of disorienting shot composition and editing provide linkages in their own endless spiral of repetition.

Music

Sergei Prokofiev's score for *Ivan the Terrible* captured this contradictory structure: the unity of repetition and disruption, the political and psychological dualisms, the freedom from form within a strictly constructed method. It is easy to see why Eisenstein was delighted with the score for *Ivan the Terrible* and deeply curious about his fellow artist's creative process. Eisenstein's work with Prokofiev stands as one of the great artistic collaborations of the twentieth century. The musical score for *Ivan the Terrible* is probably less well known than Prokofiev's score for *Alexander Nevsky*, but it is a better score cinematically. Eisenstein believed that Prokofiev had perfectly captured the structure and rhythm of the film in his music. The composer produced flawlessly attuned motifs and he uncannily replicated the film's tone of strangeness and allure and its montage-image structure. As a result, the score adds an important dimension to the expressionistic formal structure of the film, enhancing its power and deepening its meanings.[96]

As with every other aspect of the film, Eisenstein played a large role in shaping the composer's work. Prokofiev was a compliant collaborator, usually happy to follow Eisenstein's leads. The two would discuss the emotional and narrative structure of a given sequence, sometimes in great detail.[97] Prokofiev would watch the daily rushes, muttering to himself and tapping his fingers to 'memorize' the underlying dynamics of movement and editing. Then, with astonishing efficiency, he would go home and compose a score that not only matched the emotional tone of a scene but, in most cases, the exact cinematic rhythm as well. 'Prokofiev knows how to grasp the structural secret which conveys the broad meaning of the phenomenon,' Eisenstein wrote.[98] The score is never 'simple illustration', or 'mechanical coincidence' between sound and image, but rather provides a musical equivalent of Eisenstein's combination of repetition and disjuncture.[99] Each character and many themes have their own identifying musical motifs (Ivan, of course, has several), but they are deployed in ways that reflect the other structures of the film. Even when musical motifs are associated with particular characters or actions, they are used expressionistically. The appearance of a motif is rarely used as simple background to intensify suspense, for example, or cue an emotion. Like visual motifs, the musical motifs represent and reflect character traits, link characters and actions, and contain musical equivalents of contradiction.

Some motifs recur whenever a character reappears on screen, fusing with the visual image. Most obviously Ivan's power theme is repeated half a dozen times to reflect his growing power. In Part I these scenes show Ivan gaining popular support; in Part II, the power theme appears in situations where power is more contested: returning to Moscow from Alexandrova and entering the cathedral for the fiery furnace. Like the visual motifs, musical passages become more complex and more ironic as they acquire additional, often contradictory implications in Part II.

Music also signals disjunction and disorientation. One of the most common of these devices is what Eisenstein called 'enjambment', a term taken from poetry that refers to lines whose ends do not coincide with the end of a sentence.[100] An important form of temporal discontinuity, Eisenstein often continued music from one sequence into the beginning of a following shot or, conversely, began music for a shot just a fraction of a second before we see the image. And, just as the narrative is interrupted at crucial moments, the editing cuts off shots just a beat or two earlier (or later) than one expects. This disjuncture occurs within shots as well, when the musical cues do not quite coincide with their visual reference.

The 'poisoning' themes offer examples of both fusion and disjuncture of sound and image. (The following will make more sense if you read it with the film running.) The Prologue opens with some quietly pulsating strings under the adult Ivan's narration, which continue through the transitional 'black clouds', to the shot of Ivan as a child. A clarinet follows the pulsing up to a strikingly high pitch, then recedes. Next we hear Glinskaia's melodramatic cry, 'Ahhh–ah–ah–ah,' following a similar trajectory up to an equally striking high pitch. Her lines, 'They've poisoned me … I'm dying' follow the same 'melody' and then we hear the clarinet rising and falling again, much louder now in the foreground, alternating with the strings pulsing up and down in both pitch and volume. Noticeably rising and falling patterns of music are associated with several other motifs in the film, especially the *oprichniki*, echoing the rising and sinking of characters in their moves of victory and defeat. This scene, in which Ivan's mother is poisoned, is linked visually with Anastasia's poisoning, but the music is significantly *not* repeated when Anastasia is murdered. Musically, the poisoning of Glinskaia is associated with Anastasia only in Part II when Fedor meets Ivan in Anastasia's bedchamber and reveals the plot to him. In other words, Eisenstein used the repetition of this musical motif not to reiterate a simple narrative parallel, but to reinforce Ivan's inability to see Anastasia's death as a murder until the second time around; the music 'sees' the narrative from Ivan's point of view. The poisoning theme, pulsating strings and the crying clarinet, also continues after Ivan's encounter with Fedor in the bedchamber into the following shot sequence as Maliuta and the *oprichniki* drag the struggling Kolychev boyars into the courtyard. Eisenstein adds another level to the fusion by associating the murder of his mother with his own punishment (revenge) of the boyars. We saw how Ivan retaliated against the boyar Shuisky for murdering his mother and then defiling her honor in the Prologue. When we see Ivan retaliate for the second time, the music links the two murders that left Ivan abandoned, reinforcing these as two key moments in his animalistic retaliation.

A variation on this particular musical motif links several other scenes not automatically connected by visual or narrative cues. The Prologue ends with Ivan declaring his determination to rule without the boyars. A fanfare of horns punctuates his arrest of Shuisky ('Seize him!'), and is joined after the arrest by a slower variation of the pulsating strings and horns from the poisoning scene. As the focus returns to Ivan, a string passage enters that inverts the high clarinet cry of the previous scene, now sinking and rising in pitch. As it rises, the strings are joined by horns that rise and rise some more (mimicking the doubling motion: rising, pause/cut, rising further) as Ivan stands up, readjusts his tunic and asserts his power (the camera also pans up, elongating his rise). As the scene ends, the sinking/rising motif is inverted again. It is taken up and repeated by a low-register clarinet, which repeats the poisoning motif, while the pulsing strings and the punctuating drums and horns grow in volume and prominence. This motif carries us back through the 'black clouds' out of the flashback and continues while Ivan recounts his present dilemma to Filipp (that he has power and support but no friends). The expectation raised by the sinking/rising clarinet and the pulsing strings peters out. But, curiously, the same motif (sinking/rising low-register clarinet, pulsing strings and double drum beat) will be repeated in an entirely different context: when Maliuta brings Efrosinia and Vladimir the cup and invitation. The same tense expectation, as another innocent is about to mount the throne, and Ivan gets his final revenge against the boyars for the depredations of his childhood.

This brief analysis of only a few musical motifs and functions in *Ivan the Terrible* gives a good indication of the ways Eisenstein intended music to be used in film. Prokofiev's ingenious understanding of montage and his ability to translate those concepts into music add a dimension to the film that enhances every aspect of narrative and structure. The visual and narrative density of each scene are complicated and augmented by music that captures the dualism, mirroring and disorientation of the narrative, psychological and the visual devices.

The aesthetic theories and formal devices used in *Ivan the Terrible* produced a high degree of correspondence between the narrative, the psychological underpinnings and the formal structures of the film. This sort of co-ordination allows us to decipher Eisenstein's purposes and appreciate the film's extraordinary power, without diminishing the complexity at its heart. Interpenetrable layers of meaning and method, forms and identities that change shape, motifs that indicate similarities as well differences criss-cross in ways that prevent any single idea or controlling argument to dominate our perception. Just the opposite: *Ivan the Terrible* offers alternatives, slippages and a mousehole to another universe to people living in a world of restrictive institutions, suffocating surveillance and compulsory conformity. Motifs with more associations than we can track, interruptions and resurrections deep in the layers of narrative, an in-dependent side-story of shadow paths not taken, forms that change shape and merge into their opposites, all underscore the fact that in *Ivan the Terrible* nothing is what it seems, everything contains its antipode, and change is possible. Infinite associations, collapsed binary oppositions, shapes that constrain and expand, all suggest the very possibility of possibility for people forced to live underground or behind public masks and rigid public identities. Eisenstein's independent shadows and fluid musicality of forms present an alternative to mere binary exchanges that are rigid and doomed. The freedom from form offers a route out of the body to *ekstasis* and transcendence.

Immersed in the symbolic universe of *Ivan the Terrible*, it is possible to forget that Eisenstein operated in a world where movement and creativity were constrained, where state surveillance was invasive and often deadly, where the necessity of wearing public masks deformed private identity. In *Ivan*, Eisenstein invented a visual universe replete with escape routes. Through the collapse and inversion of biologically or socially restrictive roles, through the possibility of eluding pre-ordained form, through the refusal to accept rigid, definitive versions of identity or biography, he created in *Ivan* the possibility of possibility. Formal density and excess emphasize the essential contradictions of life, and show us ways in which history repeats itself in tragic cycles. But contradiction is not necessarily a dead-end. Forms offering collapse, multiplicity and diversity provide an escape from the pre-ordained and a foundation for ecstatic unity.

Philosophy and 'Unity'

'All my work is always about unity.'[101]

So Eisenstein wrote in his diary in 1943 just as he began shooting *Ivan the Terrible*. But the emphatic simplicity of the statement is misleading, for Eisenstein's concept of unity was as much about fragmentation and collision as it was about overcoming divisions, and it was anything but simple.

Ivan the Terrible comprises unity in two fundamental ways. First, the film is constructed according to principles of formal unity. As discussed above, Eisenstein believed that art could produce *ekstasis* for its viewers if it were suffused with a single unifying principle. *Ivan* is composed of recurring dialectical processes: the 'unity of opposites', multiplied many times. Second, Eisenstein explores the same dialectics that structure the film in a variety of contexts within the film's narratives. The tsar is himself a 'unity of opposites', a single, whole individual divided by contradictory desires. Ivan's inner conflicts are externalized and personified in conflicts with the people around him as well. His destructive impulses conflict internally with his constructive goals *and* his destructive impulse is externalized and embodied by Maliuta Skuratov. Ivan's egotistical will to power conflicts with his selfless devotion to the Russian state *and* this 'Caesarism' is embodied by Andrei Kurbsky. As an omnipotent adult, Ivan retains the fears of his childhood and this conflict is replicated by the powerful Efrosinia's infantilizing of her son Vladimir. In other words, the concept of unity is embedded in both the form and the content of the film: unity is Eisenstein's term for the essential dialectical process that lies at the heart of every feature of Ivan the ruler and *Ivan* the film. But all-encompassing though it is, unity never settles into something static or totalizing in Eisenstein's hands. It is important and interesting (and capable of producing *ekstasis*) only because of the ongoing tension between pairs of contradictory mirror images. The dynamic and paradoxical nature of Eisenstein's concept of unity and his ability to deploy it in so many directions at once give this film its stunning complexity and its haunting beauty.

Ivan the Terrible is a massive, fluid system of interlinked dualistic narratives, images, sounds and movements that collide in various directions, forward and backward in time, and across layers and themes. But the connections are neither mechanical nor especially systematic. As in his writing, Eisenstein liked to construct intellectual arguments by piling on examples drawn from diverse sources and contexts. His theoretical works read in parts like shopping lists: the validity of a point is demonstrated by showing the reader how often and in how many different circumstances the phenomenon under discussion appeared. Unity often functions the same way in *Ivan*. Every scene or episode, every image or gesture contains a multitude of references to other scenes, images and ideas. The viewer can enter analysis of the film at almost any point and proceed in any direction to find a network of related, but not quite symmetrical, patterns of dualism, repetition and conflict. Take, for example, the remarkable fresco that wraps around the ceiling and walls of Ivan's reception room. The composite image (intended for the Prologue) contains or suggests almost every issue raised by *Ivan*. Part archangel, part nature allegory, it unites male and female, religion and nature, the sun and the moon, power and vulnerability, birth and death, good and evil, obedience and resistance, violence and justice in one androgynous body. Fragmented body parts escape from our gaze as the fiery sun transforming gradually into a placid moon suggests the very tension between opposites unified in one body: colliding, merging, transforming. Or look at the patterns of similarity and opposition in the Coronation scenes. Ivan's initial crowning, Kurbsky's welcome in Poland, Ivan's self-anointment as 'terrible' during the fiery furnace scene, and Vladimir Staritsky's farcical masquerade all convey images of Ivan's vast power, the efforts at resistance by those around him (echoing his own internal conflicts) and their frightful submission to his will. But each scene can also ignite our imagination's flight in a variety of different directions. Images of fathers and sons evoke images of mothers and sons in one direction, fatherless brothers in another, motherless children in another, male lovers, cross-dressing androgyny, masking, betrayal, patricide and so on. Any one of those paths could take us to yet another trail of associations: bodies dividing into sexes, separating from their shadows, contorting in painful transformations; or powerless, parentless children retaliating against authority in spasms of revenge, as they simultaneously mature to adulthood and regress to a pre-logical state of animal savagery.

From history, to politics, to psychology, to aesthetics: *Ivan the Terrible* is composed of layers of dialectical cycles that intersect each other repeatedly and represent the dialectical conflicts within Ivan. Contradictions are resolved (unified) and characters strive for brief moments of *ekstasis*, only to fall apart again in the face of new conflicts. At this point the weary reader may wonder if there is a point to any of this or if it is merely a dog biting its own tail. I began this book by saying that *Ivan* is a difficult film because there are no clear boundaries between characters or even between people on and off the screen. The preceding division of my analysis into neatly contained subjects is artificial and in some ways antithetical to the spirit of the film – though a necessary tool for working our way into this labyrinth. Now it is time to examine how, and possibly why, Eisenstein composed such a dense and complex thing.

Eisenstein's dialectic differs from standard Marxist dialectics in his frankly anti-materialist attraction to the transformative moment, the ecstatic unity, over the product of the union. The almost infinite layers, repetitions and connections among dialectical processes in *Ivan* assert the validity and robustness of a dialectical view of the world, while at the same time repudiating the linear historical dialectic (from feudalism, through capitalism to socialism) favored by Russian (and other) communists. And Eisenstein, who is deeply ironic like Ivan, 'sees [everything] from two angles'.[102] Not only is Eisenstein's dialect anti-materialist, it lacks a clear commitment to the idea of historical progress. Though he believed that human cultures evolve, that societies evolve, and that the 'modern' industrial world was an improvement on 'primitive' life, the dialectic in *Ivan* seems rather ambivalent on the question of progress. Endlessly colliding and ricocheting oppositions negate the linear evolutionary progress of Marxist dialectical materialism. In their place, we find far more prevalent patterns that either cycle or rise and fall. The concepts of historical change and individual development that emerge from the piling on of dialectical 'unity of opposites' in *Ivan* suggest a world in which multiple paths of development are possible, though we often find ourselves trapped in circular, self-defeating repetition.

The cycles of violent deaths and demonic rebirths convey a dynamic and paradoxical model of individual (as well as societal) inner conflicts: not only are we divided internally but we exhibit those divisions through our efforts to efface them (or overthrow them), by repeatedly merging to create new forms, new genders, new identities, which turn out to be depressingly similar to the old ones. In enacting that dynamic, repetitive process, Eisenstein suggests, we seek to merge not only our morally or sexually divided natures but also our emotional (or infantile, pre-logical) and our evolved, intellectual abilities. All the characters in *Ivan the Terrible* have animal-like and childlike sides, which are incorporated into their thinking, plotting and planning. But abstract thought (formal adherence to both the state and the clan) and pre-logical emotionalism (the infantile Vladimir, the retaliatory young Ivan) are destructive if left on their own. The 'unity of opposites' therefore is doubly paradoxical: the unity we seek as relief from our divisions is a closed system, a dead-end, but the dualisms that torment us are necessary for the open-endedness that allows us to change, to evolve and to create.

This paradox is central to Eisenstein's conception of the 'unity of opposites' and lies at the heart of the fundamental structuring principle of the film. Unity (whether political, psychological or aesthetic) is the stated goal, but it is always elusive. The 'unity of opposites' is not a state to be reached, much less a sign of progress, but an ephemeral experience. Repetition, mirroring, pairing and re-pairing characters in cross-gender combinations illustrate the essential but shifting dualism Eisenstein found at the root of human psychology. The collisions among such doubles produced a synthesis and a higher unity through their eventual collapse and merger. But since each new 'higher unity' is as divided as its parents, the process is never-ending. The pervasiveness and dynamism of the 'unity of opposites', in Eisenstein's piling on of examples and cross-references, created a universe in which linkages (among dualistically divided souls) are so many and so complex that any kind of final unity is an ephemeral and ever-receding ideal.

'Piling on' also affects the way we perceive *Ivan the Terrible*. Throughout his career, Eisenstein thought cinema should startle viewers into feeling and thinking with emotional and intellectual intensity. *Ivan*'s sensory overload combines an appeal to the intellect and the senses. We cannot possibly grasp *Ivan* as a whole while watching it, especially the first time around. But we can experience it best if we watch it with our conscious and our subconscious together. The profusion of overlapping, patterned ideas and images addresses our perception on an intellectual and an instinctive level at the same time.

Eisenstein did not imagine that the warring sides of our personalities could be bridged or that history would ever cease to be tragically ironic. But the search for linkages was fundamental to his intellectual makeup. And he liked nothing more than to find parallels and connections, matching types of phenomenon in differing contexts. He was continually delighted to discover that historical sources proved an insight he had already reached by artistic instinct, for example.[103] But his yearning for connection went even further: 'for everything I do touches everything else, and everything crosses into everything else'.[104] Alongside *Ivan the Terrible* itself, Eisenstein's journals amply demonstrate his intellectual avidity for finding links across his wide reading. The private writings also reveal an emotional logic: as a man with few opportunities for intimacy, Eisenstein longed for connection itself. His desire for merging, for shape-changing, for exchange and mirroring, in a word, for *unity*, is a reflection of his own profound singularity and loneliness. Like Ivan, he was both divided and alone; by nature and by necessity.

The film's surface narrative tells us that Ivan was isolated by his selfless commitment to the Russian state, which cost him his friends, his wife and his family. But we have seen that he was also divided and isolated by his lingering commitment to humane values which kept him from becoming a true 'superman', for better and for worse. Throughout the film, Ivan seeks a way to embody the 'unity of opposites' in politics, morality and sexuality but when he finds escape from the confinement of his isolation and dualism, it is always accompanied by pain and contortion or violence. Only at the very end of Part III do we get a glimpse of the unity Ivan longed for: in death. His last enemy is defeated, his last friend dies, time itself is unhinged as Ivan flies wildly backward in time, and the tsar stands triumphant on the shore. 'Here – in death ... in the twinkling of one radiant moment – solitude and isolation perish.'[105] But even in death, Ivan leaves us with a puzzle: in Eisenstein's drawing of the film's finale, the waves are finished licking Ivan's feet and he is walking along the sand, deflated and head bowed, over the inscription 'Alone? ... '

At the end of *Nonindifferent Nature*, after numerous examples of the unity to be achieved after death drawn from great literature and philosophy (Tolstoy, William James, Shakespeare), Eisenstein recalls his romantic impressions of Mexico, where he found a personal, very satisfying resonance with the landscape and culture. In Eisenstein's Mexico there is:

> the constant mixture of life and death, appearance and disappearance, dying and being born – at every step ... Everywhere life forces its way out

from under death; death takes away the obsolete; centuries lie behind, but also the feeling that *nothing has yet begun*, that much is not yet finished, and that from what has just arisen – there is the possibility of everything developing ... [106]

If Ivan is seen not only as a divided individual, who found unity in death, but as the historical figure, whose work was not yet finished, then he stands at the beginning of 'the possibility of everything developing' and not alone, but at the beginning of a new dialectic. Eisenstein's final question mark is the question mark of time and the possibility of possibility. It is the ultimate symbol of the paradox and dynamism inherent in the 'unity of opposites'. And it offers us, the viewers, the only experience of unity that is possible in life: the ecstatic pathos that momentarily takes us outside ourselves. For Eisenstein, the merger of past and present, birth and death, good and evil, intellectual and emotional, the violent wrenching of ourselves out of ourselves could be found only in art. Cinema, with its ability to unite the senses, was 'the highest of all the arts'.

The last great irony of Eisenstein's *Ivan the Terrible* is that the director who is often considered the exemplar of Socialist Materialist or Socialist Realist cinema reveals himself as a psychoanalytically-oriented mystic. The revolutionary, anti-religious ideologue turned the dialectic into a tool for achieving transcendence and used Freud and Rank as models for understanding revolution. One of the film-makers most closely associated with the cult of Stalin made a film, not only about the dangers (and appeal) of demagoguery and dictatorship, but about the individual's ability to escape social reality altogether through shape-changing, merging oppositions, rebirth and *ekstasis*. But Eisenstein was no ordinary mystic; he shared Ivan's ability to see everything 'from two angles'. *Ivan the Terrible*, Eisenstein's 'self-portrait', his 'epic', reflects the director's life-long intellectual projects and his most complex thinking and his deepest desires: to merge the emotional and the intellectual, to resolve his conflicted identity and impulses, to escape from all imposed authorities and predetermined forms, to laugh at life's bizarre jokes, to acknowledge the inevitability of conflict, the deep divisions in identity, the lure of power and the transcendence of art.

But Eisenstein knew as well as anyone that art is not created in some hermetic zone of intertexuality, no matter how much he might have preferred it that way. In one of the last passages of his memoirs, Eisenstein uses the subject of 'unity' to slyly address the tension in his own career between the demands of political reality and the dictates of his imagination, the conflict between working independently and working on state commission.[107] In a circumlocution typical of his memoirs but too complex to detain us here, he rejects as irrelevant the thematic concept of unity that he identified with each of his films in published articles and public speeches: national, patriotic (*Nevsky*), socio-economic (*The Old and the New*), collective (*Potemkin*), communist (*Fergana Canal*) and, in *Ivan's* case, state unity. The deeper unity he wants to address here is to be found not in the subject matter of his films but in the creative process, specifically in the encounter between reality and artistic creativity. 'The process of assimilating material, i.e. making it "one's own", happens at the moment when, coming into contact with reality, it begins to set itself out according to a grid of outlines and sketches of the same special structure as that in which one's consciousness was formed.'[108] This 'reality' is still rather abstract, but it becomes clearer when he introduces a metaphor found in Leonardo da Vinci, with whom Eisenstein self-flatteringly has always compared himself. Producing films, he tells us, is something like the 'complex knots' designed by Leonardo for the ceiling of the Milan Academy.

> We encounter a phenomenon.
> And the plan of this knot seems to be laid over this phenomenon.
> The features of one coincide, or otherwise.
> They coincide partially.
> Here and There.
> They do not coincide.
> They clash with one another striving for coincidence.[109]

At first this passage seems to be about varieties of unity or about adapting historical reality to artistic requirements: Eisenstein often reminds us to look beneath the surface (in this case, the surface knot) for the real story. But here the layers of Leonardo's knot hint at yet another unity connected with the 'state unity' Eisenstein has just dethroned. The surfaces and depths here introduce a conflict between a phenomenon and its *official* representation. The two layers struggle, striving for some kind of 'coincidence', a more limited word than 'unity'. (An artist negotiating the space between his own creativity and the demands of his patron is not searching for unity, just peaceful coexistence.) Eyeing the gulf between them, the artist knows something will have to be sacrificed. Eisenstein ends the chapter defiantly, if rather furtively. When, in his career, reality has conflicted with his artistic goals, he says that he often violated reality to preserve the integrity of his 'individual desire', but, 'he cannot actually remember any examples' of violating art to satisfy the demands of reality.[110] However accurate that assessment in fact, Eisenstein ends his memoirs with a defiant claim for the autonomy of art and the chapter as a whole shows his acknowledgment of the tension between external demands and individual desires in his work.

Eisenstein's defense of artistic integrity seems at first to contradict statements quoted earlier that he had 'on several occasions to stoop to such levels of self-abasement ... perhaps too frequently, too hastily, and almost too willingly'.[111] But this collision is not exactly a contradiction. The two passages taken together show us the devil's bargain Eisenstein made and the painful 'unity of opposites' it created within him. After a decade of frustrated attempts to make the films he wanted to make, he was willing to 'violate reality' and abase himself in order to ensure *Ivan*'s completion. He wrote the required articles of explanation and self-criticism, he performed the role of cultural luminary when required to do so by his state patrons, but at the same time he fought off political and bureaucratic efforts to deform the film he wanted to make. He shot more scenes than he thought he would be able to use, he accepted some cuts, and fought hard to preserve scenes central to his aims. But the trade-off was never simple and the price Eisenstein paid, in shame and self-doubt, was high. Ivan's burning question, 'Am I doing the right thing?', his plaintive justifications, and his burning confession, 'It is agonizing to build a state at such a price,' were Eisenstein's own questions and justifications. Does the end justify the means? That remains an open question.

Notes

1. 1923/2/1165/4 [4 Apr. 1941].
2. On Stalin's Ivan project see D. Brandenberger, *National Bolshevism: Stalinist Mass Culture and the Formation of Modern Russian National Identity, 1931–1956*, Cambridge, 2002; and M. Perrie, *The Cult of Ivan the Terrible in Stalin's Russia*, Basingstoke and New York, 2001.
3. A balanced introduction to Ivan's reign can be found in J. Martin, *Medieval Russian History, 980–1584*, Cambridge, 1995.
4. '*Ivan the Terrible*: A Film About the Sixteenth-century Russian Renaissance', *ESW 3*, p. 191.
5. 1923/1/552/55 (in English in the original, spelling corrected).
6. *Beyond the Stars, ESW 4*, p. 453.
7. Aesthetic and cinematic devices will be discussed below.
8. It is worth noting here that Eisenstein intended the triumph in Part I to be stained by the darker themes of violence and vengeance contained in two scenes that were cut by censors: the 'Prologue' and the 'Oath of the Oprichniki'.

9. Holy Fools were well known but vaguely defined characters in pre-modern Russian culture. Often considered to have a special spiritual sensibility and moral authority by virtue of their eccentric or other-worldly demeanor and their outsider status, they defied social and political norms for reasons ranging from political defiance to some form of mental incapacity.

10. 1923/1/552/36; 1923/2/124/26; 1923/2/128/1 [18 Feb. 1943].

11. 1923/2/128/2 [19 Mar. 1943].

12. This was a key scene for Eisenstein in his analysis of the film's structure; see *NN*, pp. 310–26.

13. 1923/2/125/2.

14. 1923/2/124/8 [16 Sept. 1941];1923/2/125/6–8.

15. 1923/2/1166/43 [11 Sept. 1943].

16. Naum Kleiman, *Neizvestnyi 'Ivan Groznyi'*, video CD, Moscow, 1998; *KZ* 38 (1998), pp. 246–53.

17. 1923/2/1175/6 [18 Apr. 1946] (in English in the original).

18. 'Ivan Groznyi: Kino-stsenarii', *Novyi mir*, pp. 80–1.

19. 1923/2/1168/6, 8 [13 Feb. 1942]; 1923/2/125/2; 1923/1/561/67.

20. 2456/1/957/10.

21. 1923/2/1172/8–9 [7 Jan. 1944]. The autobiographical and psychoanalytical issues will be discussed in more detail below.

22. 1923/2/1172/9 [7 Jan. 1944].

23. 1923/1/127/1–3 [3 Mar. 1942].

24. 'Stalin, Molotov and Zhdanov on *Ivan the Terrible* Part Two', *ESW 3*, pp. 300–1.

25. Ibid., pp. 299–300.

26. Kleiman, *Neizvestnyi 'Ivan Groznyi'*.

27. J. A. Getty and O. V. Naumov (eds), *The Road to Terror*, New Haven, CT, 2002; L. Siegelbaum and A. Sokolov (eds), *Stalinism as a Way of Life* (eds), New Haven, CT, 2000.

28. 1923/2.128/33 [23 Nov. 43]; Naum Kleiman, 'Formula finala', *KZ* 38 (1998), pp. 100–32.

29. *NN*, p. 324.

30. '*Ivan the Terrible*: A Film', *ESW 3*, p. 191.

31. 1923/2/1166/19–25 [8 Oct. 1941]; 1923/1/561/4 [9 Mar. 1941], 1923/1/561/28 [Aug. 1942].

32. *NN*, pp. 323–5; for more on circles and wheels, see Kristin Thompson, *Eisenstein's Ivan the Terrible*, Princeton, NJ, 1981.

33. 1923/1/569/61 [20 Apr. 1941]; *NN*, pp. 325–6.

34. *NN*, pp. 323–6.

35. This diary entry is Eisenstein's linkage of Ivan's symbolic unifying force with the *Battleship Potemkin*'s symbolic unification of images; 1923/2/1169/5–6 [2 Apr. 1942].

36. 1923/2/124/56–7 [16 Sept. 1941].

37. 1923/2/124/13 [16 Sept. 1941].

38. *NN*, p. 105. It is worth noting that in the screenplay where Eisenstein alludes to Belinsky's description, he omits the reference to 'madness'; see *IP*, vol. 6, p. 379; *Ivan the Terrible*, Montagu and Marshall (eds and trans.), p. 236.

39. Perrie, *The Cult of Ivan*, pp. 78–102.

40. A survey of the historians that Eisenstein read can be found in Robert Crummey, 'Ivan the Terrible', in *Windows on the Russian Past*, S. Baron and N. Heer (eds), Columbus, OH, 1977 and Perrie, *The Cult of Ivan*, pp. 6–11.

41. K. D. Kavelin, 'Vzgliad na iuridicheskii byt drevnei Rossii', *Sobranie sochinenii*, vol. 1, St Petersburg, 1897, p. 47.

42. '*Ivan the Terrible*: A Film', *ESW 3*, p. 189.

43. *NN*, p. 310.

44. 'Stalin, Molotov and Zhdanov', *ESW 3*, pp. 300–1.

45. 1923/2/1168/28 [4 Oct. 1942].

46. In particular, *Molotov Remembers. Conversations wih Felix Chuyev*, Chicago, 1993.

47. Ian Christie, 'Ivan Groznyi', *Monthly Film Bulletin*, vol. 54, no. 647 (December 1987).

48. *Beyond the Stars, ESW 4*, p. 125.

49. Ibid., p. 126.

50. 1923/1/554/31 [21 Feb. 1942]; 1923/2/1172/9ob. [7 Jan. 1944]. On the Freudian and Oedipal nature of this relationship and its social analogs, see also V. V. Ivanov, *Ocherki po istorii semiotiki v SSSR*, Moscow, 1976, pp. 98ff.

51. 1923/2/1168/22 [26 Feb. 1942].

52. On Meierkhol'd's image in *Ivan*, see L. Kozlov, 'A Hypothetical Dedication', *Eisenstein Revisited*, L. Kleberg and H. Lövgren (eds), Stockholm, 1987, pp. 65–92.

53. *Beyond the Stars, ESW 4*, pp. 424–53; 1923/2/1167/33–41 [16 Nov. 41].

54. *Dessins Secrets*, Paris, 1999.

55. *Beyond the Stars, ESW 4*, pp. 739–42.

56. Ibid., p. 742.

57. Ibid., p. 739.

58. Formal elements of such transformations will be discussed below.

59. Otto Rank, *The Trauma of Birth*, New York, 1993 (original publication, 1924).

60. *Beyond the Stars. ESW 4*, p. 501.

61. Yuri Tsivian, *Ivan the Terrible*, London and Berkley, CA, 2002, pp. 77–80.

62. *Beyond the Stars, ESW 4*, p. 434.

63. *NN*, pp. 312–13, 323–4.

64. *Beyond the Stars. ESW 4*, p. 506.

65. 1923/2/1168/7 [13 Feb. 1942].

66. S. M. Eizenshtein, *Izbrannye proizvedeniia v shesti tomakh*, vol. 6, Moscow, 1971, p. 510. A partial translation of these notes can be found in N. M. Lary, *Dostoevsky and Soviet Film: Visions of Demonic Realism*, Ithaca, NY, 1986, pp. 242–54.

67. Cited in V. V. Ivanov, 'The Semiotic Theory of Carnival as the Inversion of

Bipolar Opposites', *Carnival!*, Thomas Seboek (ed.), Berlin, 1984, pp. 12–15; also, *Beyond the Stars, ESW 4*, pp. 604–9.

68. Thompson, *Eisenstein's Ivan the Terrible*, p. 202.
69. Expressionism, camerawork, and other elements of form in *Ivan the Terrible* are discussed in detail in Thompson, *Eisenstein's Ivan the Terrible*; see also David Bordwell, *The Cinema of Eisenstein*, Cambridge, MA, pp. 233–53; Tsivian, *Ivan the Terrible*.
70. The concept of *ostranenie*, or 'making it strange', was introduced by the Russian formalist critic Viktor Shklovskii; see 'Art as Technique', *Russian Formalist Criticism: Four Essays*, L. T. Lemon and M. J. Rice (eds and transl.), Lincoln, NE, 1965.
71. 1923/1/554/62 [21 Jan. 41].
72. Tsivian, 'Eisenstein's Visual Vocabulary' (DVD audiovisual essay), *Eisenstein: The Sound Years*.
73. *NN*, pp. 302, 305, 327.
74. Bordwell, *The Cinema of Eisenstein*, p. 190.
75. *NN*, pp. 123–53.
76. 1923/2/124/30 [31 Mar. 1942].
77. 1923/2/124/28–30 [30–31 Mar. 1942].
78. Thompson, *Eisenstein's Ivan the Terrible*, pp. 188–91; Tsivian, *Ivan the Terrible*, pp. 30–2.
79. 1923/1/561/128 [Mar. 1942]; I. Grabar', *Istoriia russkogo iskusstva*, vol. VI, Moscow, 1909, p. 320.
80. Grabar', *Istoriia russkogo iskusstva*, p. 322.
81. 1923/1/569/45 [23 Aug. 1941].
82. 'The Problem of the Materialist Approach to Form', *ER*, p. 59.
83. 1923/1/553/103 [Feb. 1941].
84. Eisenstein shared with Bakhtin such ideas about surveillance and identity.
85. *Eisenstein on Disney*, Jay Leyda (ed.), Alan Upchurch (trans.), Calcutta, 1986. For more on eyes, see Thompson, *Eisenstein's Ivan the Terrible*, pp. 114–29, 163–5.
86. On cross-dressing and identity see Anne Nesbet, 'Inanimations: Snow White and Ivan the Terrible', *Film Quarterly*, vol. 50, no. 4, pp. 20–31.
87. On shadows and the possibility of possibility see Gary Saul Morson, *Narrative and Freedom: The Shadow of Time*, New Haven, CT, 1994.
88. *Eisenstein on Disney*, pp. 2, 4, 21.
89. Ibid., pp. 57–9; Nesbet, 'Inanimations', pp. 24–5.
90. This scene and the evolution of polyphonic montage from *Potemkin* to *Ivan* are discussed in *NN*, pp. 293–328. My analysis of it differs slightly from Eisenstein's.
91. *NN*, pp. 305, 327.
92. On axial cutting see D. Bordwell, 'Eisenstein, Socialist Realism, and the Charms of Mizanstsena', *Eisenstein at 100: A Reconsideration*, A. Lavalley and B. P. Scherr (eds), New Burnswick, NJ, 2001, pp. 13–37.

93. 1923/1/554/20 [6 Sep. 41]; 1923/2/128 [8 May 43].

94. 'From Lectures on Music and Color in *Ivan the* Terrible', *ESW 3*, p. 326.

95. In his notes, Eisenstein made it clear that his conception of the film's structure was neither purely formal nor entirely aesthetically motivated, but was intended to correspond to the film 'thematically and psychologically'. 1923/2/128/27–9 [8 May 1943].

96. 'PRKFV', *NFD*, pp. 149–67.

97. 'Lectures on Music and Color', *ESW 3*, pp. 317–22.

98. 'PRKFV', p. 163.

99. Ibid., pp. 157, 163.

100. *NN*, p. 327. On other sound disjunctures, see Thompson, *Eisenstein's Ivan the Terrible*, pp. 275–81.

101. 1923/2/128/32.

102. 1923/1/553/103.

103. 1923/1/553/9.

104. 1923/2/268/37 [17 Nov. 1947].

105. *NN*, p. 363.

106. *NN*, pp. 380, 382.

107. *Beyond the Stars*, *ESW 4*, pp. 787–95.

108. Ibid., p. 794.

109. Ibid. The two layers of Leonardo's knot also represent a central concept in Eisenstein's theoretical work, the relationship between the image and its representation; see Bordwell, *The Cinema of Eisenstein*, pp. 163–77.

110. *Beyond the Stars*, *ESW 4*, p. 795.

111. Ibid., pp. 741–2.

3. Synopsis

This synopsis is based on the most recent definitive version of *Ivan the Terrible* available.[1] It describes all scenes included in the final *released* versions of Parts I and II. It also includes short descriptions of scenes cut from the released versions if I have been able to view or reconstruct them.[2] The synopsis of Part III is based on the original screenplay and the few recovered fragments of scenes shot for Part III.[3]

Ivan the Terrible, Part I

The film opens with an abstract shot of billowing storm clouds against threatening music, and titles which read: 'This film is the story of the man who was the first to unite our country, the Grand Prince of Moscow who united greedy, warring and divided principalities into a single, powerful State, the military leader who made the glory of Russian arms resound in the East and the West, the sovereign who resolved his country's cruel dilemmas by crowning himself tsar of all Rus.'

Ivan's coronation at age seventeen takes place in the Uspensky Cathedral in Moscow's Kremlin. Before Ivan enters we meet his fiancée Anastasia and his supporters as well as his various political enemies, international and domestic intriguers. Ivan crowns himself. His two friends, Andrei Kurbsky and Fedor Kolychev, anoint him in a shower of golden coins. Ivan announces his plan to make Russia an international power by constructing the Great Russian State and reclaiming ancient Russian lands, which alienates everyone in the hall: the boyars, the Church and foreign dignitaries react with varying degrees of fear and anger. The sinister Livonian Ambassador tempts Prince Kurbsky to wonder why he should not be tsar instead of Ivan.

Ivan and Anastasia are married. His one happy moment is marred by the betrayal of his friends. Kolychev chooses to enter a monastery rather than serve a tsar whose policies he opposes; he becomes the priest Filipp. Kurbsky has yet to openly betray Ivan, but we learn that he covets both Ivan's wife and his throne. The wedding is interrupted by the arrival of an angry mob, seeking the heads of the wealthy boyars. The boyars scatter and Ivan imperiously approaches the men, who cower at the sight of him. He pacifies the crowd. Maliuta Skuratov, who led the attack and tried to kill the tsar, has been completely won over and will become Ivan's most faithful servant.

This scene is interrupted by the arrival of ambassadors from Kazan, the last stronghold of the Mongol (also known as Tatar) rulers who had occupied Russian lands for two hundred years. The ambassador threatens Ivan, but the tsar rises to the challenge, claiming that Russia will defeat Kazan once and for all. He rallies the crowd, now transformed from an angry revolutionary mob into a patriotic fighting force with the cry 'To Kazan!'

The battle scenes in Kazan establish the tsar's preeminence and Russia's victory, but they also suggest some of the picture's darker themes. Maliuta Skuratov continues his rise from rebel leader to loyal servitor by tunneling under the Kazan fortress and using explosives to destroy it, which wins the battle. Ivan also discovers the commoner Alexei Basmanov at Kazan; Basmanov warns him against the boyars. Kurbsky punishes the Mongol prisoners with a cruelty that Ivan deplores. They argue; Kurbsky raises his hand to the tsar, but his shield inadvertently saves Ivan's life by deflecting an arrow aimed at Ivan's heart: treachery and loyalty intertwined.

We return to the Kremlin to find Ivan on his deathbed, creating a dynastic crisis. If Ivan dies, his successor is a tiny baby, Dmitri, depicted angelically in Anastasia's arms. Efrosinia sees her chance to persuade the boyars to pledge their loyalty to her son Vladimir instead. Is the tsar really sick or is this a ploy to uncover the conspiracy? Kurbsky is tempted by Efrosinia and by the possibility that Anastasia might be free to marry. Kurbsky and Anastasia meet furtively with Maliuta Skuratov watching from the shadows. After secretly promising Efrosinia to pledge his allegiance to Vladimir, Kurbsky learns that the tsar is recovering and reaffirms his pledge to Ivan.

The boyars bemoan the appointment of commoners like Alexei Basmanov to important positions. Others arrive with word of massive arrests. Pimen, the Metropolitan of Moscow, has been demoted to Archbishop of Novgorod. Efrosinia, undaunted, is determined to undermine Ivan.

She plots to destroy him by poisoning his wife Anastasia, who has become ill.

Ivan bemoans Russia's weakness in the West and the need for control of the Baltic coast. He sits at a chessboard which he uses to illustrate his hopes for an alliance with England. He sends his ambassador, Nepeya, there with instructions that Ivan alone has the authority to negotiate.

Ivan goes to Anastasia's bedchamber feeling abandoned and alone; she comforts him. Efrosinia leaves a goblet with poisoned wine right where Ivan will reach for it when Anastasia needs a drink. Anastasia drinks from the cup, seeming to know what Ivan does not, that she has been poisoned.

The climax to Part I occurs as personal sorrow and political betrayal come. A grief-stricken Ivan mourns at his wife's coffin. In a corner of the cathedral, Pimen reads from the sixty-eighth Psalm, a dispiriting lament about loneliness and abandonment. From the other corner, Maliuta lists the boyars who have abandoned Moscow and rejected Ivan's quest to build the Great Russian State. Ivan begins to doubt himself and his cause. Alexei Basmanov arrives with his son Fedor and the worst news: Kurbsky has gone over to the enemy and is raising an army to fight against Ivan. Shattered by this news, Ivan gathers his resolve, sends Pimen from the cathedral and reaffirms his commitment to the Great Russian State. Basmanov suggests Ivan create his own army of men chosen from the people, devoted to Ivan and his cause. Basmanov offers Ivan his own son, Fedor, for the army. Ivan likes the idea. He resolves to leave Moscow and step down from the throne; if the people come to request that he return to rule over them, he will know that his is the right path. The scene ends with the incarnation of the new army in a flood of young men in black and carrying black candles hailing Ivan as he stands astride the coffin arms uplifted. He kisses Anastasia goodbye.

An official reads a proclamation announcing the tsar's abandonment of Moscow. Those humble men who are ready to serve the tsar faithfully are summoned to join his new Oprichnik Guard in Alexandrova Sloboda.

A scene, 'The Oath of the *Oprichniki*', was cut here. Young men take a solemn oath to the tsar and to the Great Russian State above all bonds of human kinship, above their bonds to their mothers and fathers, their friends and brothers.

After the oath, Ivan sits disheartened as he and his devoted servitor Maliuta wait to see if the people will come to him. Finally in the distance a snaking line of people is seen making its way to the palace to beg Ivan to return to Moscow and rule again. Ivan goes out solemnly to greet them.

Ivan the Terrible, **Part II: The Boyars' Plot**

Part II begins with a recap of Part I in selected scenes with voiceover.
The action begins in the Polish King Sigismund's throne room. Kurbsky seals his act of treachery by offering Sigismund his allegiance in a
ceremonial sword ritual. He conveys messages he has received that testify
to Ivan's current weakness. Sigismund represents himself as an outpost
of European civilization in contrast to Muscovite barbarism and swears
to destroy Russian unity in order to protect Europe from the savage
Russians. A herald appears with news that Ivan is not weak but is
returning to Moscow to take up the throne again. Kurbsky is dismayed.

Ivan and his *oprichniki* thunder across the snowy landscape to Moscow.
Ivan enters the palace and chastises the boyars. He announces the establishment of his *oprichnina*: the portion of land that he will keep as his
own private domain, and of the elite guard he has created, the *oprichniki*.
He says he will protect Russia's borders and eradicate treason. His old
friend Kolychev, now the priest Filipp, is the only one with the nerve to
challenge Ivan's plans openly. Ivan embraces Filipp and ushers him off
to talk. Ivan asks why the priest is so harsh. Ivan explains himself with
a flashback to his childhood.

Eisenstein intended the scenes of childhood to be set at the beginning
of Part I. A young Ivan sits alone in a dark antechamber; his mother,
Elena Glinskaia, warns him against the boyars, who have poisoned her
and drag her away from the terrified, orphaned Ivan. A harrowing scene
cut from the released version casts doubt on Ivan's legitimacy by showing
the hunting down and killing of Glinskaia's lover, Ivan Telepnev, with
Ivan watching helplessly in terror. Next we see Ivan timidly enter the tsar's
throne room in the Golden Palace. Real power is exercised by the boyars
who are negotiating a trade treaty. Two boyars, Shuisky and Belsky, argue
about whom they should pay for a trading treaty. They are still arguing
back in Ivan's bedchamber as servants remove the boy's royal garments.
Ivan suddenly asserts his will, claiming that Russia will pay no one. The
boyars laugh; Russia is too weak. After Shuisky lies down on Ivan's
mother's bed, Ivan surprises everyone by ordering Shuisky to be arrested.
It is the first time Ivan uses his power and he likes it. Ivan announces that
he will rule alone without the boyars, that he *will* be tsar. End of flashback.

Ivan begs Filipp to stay by his side. Since becoming tsar he has been
betrayed by all around him and deprived of his wife: he is *alone,* and
crushed by the burdens of power. Filipp refuses. Ivan gives in to Filipp's
demand that he be allowed to save his innocent Kolychev relatives
accused of treason. Filipp withdraws.

Enter Maliuta, who unlike Filipp serves the tsar as faithfully as a dog and loves him unconditionally. Maliuta persuades Ivan that he can keep his word to Filipp and still execute Filipp's Kolychev kin as planned, by using Maliuta to do the dirty deed. As Maliuta withdraws we see Ivan in doubt and anguish. He looks heavenward and asks whether he has the right to judge other men.

Ivan hears a cry but instead of running to the execution site he retreats to his dead wife's bedroom. Fedor Basmanov, who also loves Ivan, helps the tsar figure out that Efrosinia had murdered Anastasia, but Ivan is reluctant to believe it.

Oprichniki drag members of the Kolychev family to the executioner's courtyard, where Maliuta reads their death sentences and beheads them. Ivan appears, slowly gazing at the corpses, looking stricken with fear and doubt. He bows before the dead, then his demeanor changes suddenly; he points to the corpses and whispers, 'Too few!'

Over the coffins of the Kolychevs, surrounded by the remaining boyars and clergy, Pimen and Efrosinia persuade Filipp to put aside his religious obligations and seek revenge for the murder of his kin for the good of all the boyars. The conspiracy proceeds, first symbolically and then literally.

Filipp tries to shame Ivan into repentance by arranging the performance of an ancient play, *The Fiery Furnace*, in which innocent children are sentenced to die for their opposition to the oppressive ruler, Nebuchadnezzar. Midway through the performance, Ivan enters. Ivan asks Filipp for his blessing, but Filipp rebuffs him and demands that Ivan submit to the authority of the Church. Just then, a small child in the audience points to Ivan, recognizing him as 'the terrible and godless tsar' of the play. Ivan notices Efrosinia and her look confirms the suspicion that she poisoned Anastasia. In response to Filipp, the child and Efrosinia, Ivan vows, 'I will be what you call me: I *will* be Terrible.'

News of Filipp's arrest shifts the plan for revenge into a higher gear. Pimen and Efrosinia plot to assassinate the tsar and seat Vladimir on the throne. Efrosinia sings her son a lullaby to persuade the terrified and reluctant Vladimir to help Peter Volynets, who is much more eager to wield the fatal knife. Maliuta appears, frightening Efrosinia and Vladimir who had been discussing the plan. He bears an invitation to the tsar's banquet and a sinister gift: the empty goblet that had been used to poison Anastasia.

In the banquet hall (shot in color), the *oprichniki* whirl and stamp in a celebration of violence. Fedor Basmanov, dressed to resemble Anastasia, leads the men in dance and song. Ivan, Vladimir, Alexei Basmanov and

Maliuta sit drunkenly at the table. Ivan tricks Vladimir into revealing the assassination plans and then tricks him into dressing in the tsar's robes, so that he, Vladimir, will be killed in Ivan's place. Vladimir, who finds that he likes sitting in the tsar's throne, is escorted through the hall by the *oprichniki* now dressed in black monks' robes. When Vladimir leaves the banquet hall, the film switches back to black-and-white; he passes through a small doorway under an icon of Christ and into the cathedral where he is stabbed by Peter. Efrosinia strides in expecting to find Ivan dead and her son the new tsar. Her discovery that Vladimir has already been 'crowned' and killed stuns her, and she repeats the creepy lullaby she sang earlier. Vladimir is dragged away. Ivan hails his would-be assassin Peter as his savior. Ivan and the *oprichniki* file past Efrosinia to the altar of the cathedral. A chorus sings of vengeance for the traitors and the *oprichniki* repeat their inhuman oath. Ivan bows before the altar, lifts his face to heaven and says, 'For the sake of Great Russian State.'

Ivan sits on the carved throne in the banquet hall surrounded by *oprichniki*. He says a tsar must show mercy to the good and cruelty to the wicked. Now that the enemies of Russian unity are defeated, his hands are free to use the Sword of Justice against Russia's external enemies.

Ivan the Terrible, Part III

Prince Kurbsky is writing to Ivan, vacillating between rage at Ivan's bloodletting and faith that Ivan had acted properly in his position. He is plotting the rebellion of Novgorod and Pskov against Ivan. Heinrich Staden, a German *oprichnik* and double agent, enters and is sent by Kurbsky to Ivan's court.

Ivan is writing to Kurbsky, angry at his betrayal and grieving the loss of friendship. Peter, the former assassin but now a loyal supporter, reveals the details of the assassination. Evstafi, Ivan's confessor, calls a little too passionately for the punishment of the rebels. Ivan organizes a campaign against Novgorod. In order to prevent any spies from revealing the plot he calls for the total annihilation of the region.

An extant scene shows Staden arriving at Ivan's library. Before an audience of appreciative *oprichniki*, Ivan cunningly toys with Staden, questioning his identity and loyalty, threatening to arrest him, then laughing at this 'joke'.

Ivan travels with his troops to Novgorod. The countryside is strewn with corpses. Maliuta is sent to Tver to kill Filipp. Ivan arrives in Novgorod in time to uncover the conspiracy led by Pimen and has Pimen arrested.

The climax of Part III is Ivan's confession in the cathedral in Novgorod. A monk reads aloud a list of those who have been killed in the campaign to construct the Great Russian State, beginning with the Staritskys and going on to those killed in the suppression of Novgorod and Pskov. Ivan is stretched out on the floor in despair and doubt in his Great Cause. He begs God to excuse his terrible deeds, but God is silent. In another part of the cathedral, Fedor Basmanov discovers that his father, together with Staden and other *oprichniki*, have been stealing from the state to enrich their own families. Ivan proceeds to banging his head on the cathedral floor until bloody. He wants to confess, but discovers that his confessor Evstafi, is a Kolychev in disguise and a traitor. Anger shakes him out of his doubt. He uses this discovery to set a trap for Kurbsky.

Both King Sigismund and Ivan, wanting an alliance with England, try to court Queen Elizabeth. A rowdy scene at her palace depicts Elizabeth as a crafty ruler, who uses both deception and sexual appeal in ruling. She deceives the emissary from Poland into thinking she is offering him an alliance, when in fact she will support Russia in Ivan's aim to take the Livonian coast.

At another feast, Ivan announces that there are traitors among the *oprichniki*. He forces Fedor to execute his father. Alexei accepts his fate but first demands that Fedor revoke his oath to the tsar and promise to preserve the family's power and wealth. Reluctantly Fedor agrees. When he returns to the banquet hall, Ivan seems to know of Fedor's last promise to his father and has Fedor killed, but not before Fedor warns Ivan about Staden's treachery.

Ivan advances towards the final battle. Kurbsky falls for Ivan's trap but he escapes and retreats to the castle at Wolmar. Maliuta finds his empty armor. Ivan rides forward, seeming to become a decade younger as he rides. The Russian forces attack Kurbsky and his allies at the castle of Weissenstein, but Kurbsky has fled on horseback. The Livonians begin exploding gunpowder in a last effort to trap the Russians. Maliuta is wounded. Ivan reaches him and carries him on a stretcher to catch a glimpse of the sea, now in Russian hands. Ivan reaches the sea. Smoke rises from battles all along the shore. The sea obeys Ivan's command. Ivan walks along the beach, alone.

Notes

1. *Eisenstein: The Sound Years. Ivan the Terrible*, Parts I and II, New York: Criterion Collection, 2001.

2. Naum Kleiman, *Neizvestnyi 'Ivan Groznyi'*, video CD.

3. An English translation of the shooting script, which conforms closely to current released versions of Parts I and II, is *Ivan the Terrible*, I. Montagu and H. Marshall (trans. and eds), London and Boston, 1989.

Bibliography

The best way to view *Ivan the Terrible* is on the DVD *Eisenstein: The Sound Years* issued by the Criterion Collection, New York, 2001.

Since this volume is primarily for readers of English, the following list focuses on English-language publications. Readers of Russian can consult a thorough bibliography in *Kinovedcheskie zapiski* [Film Studies Notes], vol. 38 (1999), a volume devoted to *Ivan the Terrible*.

Works by Eisenstein

Eisenstein on Disney, Jay Leyda (ed.), Alan Upchurch (trans.), Calcutta, 1986.

The Eisenstein Reader, Richard Taylor (ed.), William Powell (trans.), London, 1988.

Ivan the Terrible [screenplay], Ivor Montagu and Herbert Marshall (trans. and eds), London and Boston, 1989.

Nonindifferent Nature, Herbert Marshall (trans.), Cambridge, 1987.

Notes of a Film Director, New York, 1970.

Risunki. Dessins. Drawings, Moscow, 1961.

Selected Works: Vol 3. Writings, 1934–47, Richard Taylor (ed.), William Powell (trans.) London, 1996.

Selected Works: Vol 4. Beyond the Stars. The Memoirs of Sergei Eisenstein, Richard Taylor (ed.), William Powell (trans.), London and Calcutta, 1996.

Works About *Ivan the Terrible*

Amengual, Barthelemy, *Que viva Eisenstein!*, Lausanne, 1980.

Aumont, Jacques, *Montage Eisenstein*, Paris, 1979.

Barthes, Roland, *S/Z*, Richard Miller (trans.), New York, 1974.

Bordwell, David, *The Cinema of Eisenstein*, Cambridge, MA, 1993.

Bulgakowa, Oksana, *Sergei Eisenstein. A Biography*, Berlin and San Francisco, 2002.

Goodwin, James, *Eisenstein, Cinema and History*, Urbana, IL, 1993.

Kozlov, Leonid, 'The Artist and the Shadow of Ivan', *Stalinism and Soviet Cinema*, Richard Taylor and Derek Spring (eds), London and New York, 1993.

— 'A Hypothetical Dedication', *Eisenstein Revisited*, L. Kleberg and H. Lövgren (eds), Stockholm, 1987.

Leyda, Jay, *Kino. A History of Russian and Soviet Film*, Princeton, NJ, 1983.

Lövgren, Hakan, *Eisenstein's Labyrinth*, Stockholm, 1996.

Nesbet, Anne, 'Inanimations: Snow White and Ivan the Terrible', *Film Quarterly*, vol. 50, no. 4 (Summer 1997).

— '*Ivan the Terrible* and The Juncture of Beginning and End', *Eisenstein at 100. A Reconsideration*, A. Lavalley and Barry Scherr (eds), New Brunswick, NJ, 2001.

Neuberger, Joan, 'The Politics of Bewilderment. *Ivan the Terrible* in 1945', *Eisenstein at 100. A Reconsideration*.

Oudart, Jean-Pierre, 'Sur *Ivan le Terrible*', *Cahiers du Cinema*, no. 218 (March 1970).

Perrie, Maureen, *The Cult of Ivan the Terrible in Stalin's Russia*, Basingstoke and New York, 2001.

Roberge, Gaston, *Eisenstein's Ivan the Terrible. An Analysis*, Calcutta, 1980.

Thompson, Kristin, *Eisenstein's Ivan the Terrible*, Princeton, NJ, 1981.

Tsivian, Yuri, *Ivan the Terrible*, London and Berkeley, 2002.

Uhlenbruch, Bernd, 'The Annexation of History: Eisenstein and the Ivan Grozny Cult in the 1940s', *The Culture of the Stalin Period*, Hans Günther (ed.), London, 1990.